# OPERA IN CENTRAL CITY

ALLEN YOUNG

SPECTROGRAPHICS, INC.
3115 E. 40th Avenue
DENVER, COLORADO 80205

Copyright 1993 by Allen Young

All rights reserved. No part of this book may be reproduced or transmitted in any form or by any means, electronic or mechanical, including photocopying, recording, or by any information storage and retrieval system, without the written permission of the publisher, except by a reviewer quoting brief passages in a magazine, newspaper or broadcast. Address inquiries to Allen Young, Box 288, 191 University Boulevard, Denver, Colorado 80206.

ISBN 0-9637541-0-6

Publisher's Cataloguing in Publication

Young, Allen, 1918
    Opera in Central City/ Allen Young
    1. History of Central City Opera House Association;
    2. Chronicle of opera and theater productions since 1932

Cover design by Barbara Young

# CONTENTS

Acknowledgements .................................................................................. 1

Daring and Imagination ............................................................................ 3

The Ricketson Years ................................................................................ 22

The Hungarian ........................................................................................ 28

The Ballad of Baby Doe .......................................................................... 36

Tosca and Others .................................................................................... 42

Merrill's Debut ........................................................................................ 44

The Ford Foundation and a Lady .......................................................... 53

Travails .................................................................................................... 56

A New Start ............................................................................................. 67

The Darling Years ................................................................................... 79

The Moriarty Years ................................................................................. 97

Illustrations follow page ......................................................................... 66

Central City Opera Repertory ............................................................... 115

# ACKNOWLEDGEMENTS

That portion of my life which has been filled by opera at Central City is a large one and one which has given many riches to my experiences in the musical life of Colorado.

There I made my first theatrical acquaintance with Mozart's *The Marriage of Figaro* and *Cosi Fan Tutte*, Beethoven's *Fidelio*, Donizetti's *Don Pasquale* and *The Elixir of Love*, Rossini's *Italian Girl in Algiers*, Verdi's *A Masked Ball*, Gounod's *Romeo and Juliet*. There I attended rehearsals and the premiere of *The Ballad of Baby Doe*.

There I heard great singers. Eleanor Steber, Regina Resnick, Judith Raskin, Beverly Sills, Norman Treigle, Cornell MacNeil, Frances Bible, and Benita Valente.

The fine directorial work of Herbert Graf, Elemer Nagy, Nathaniel Merrill, William Francisco was to be seen there as was the superb design work of Donald Oenslager, Robert O'Hearn, and Robert Darling as well as Nagy.

There I saw superb theater with Helen Hayes, Katharine Cornell, Lillian Gish, Shirley Booth, Julie Harris, Maurice Evans, Louis Calhern, Sir Michael Redgrave, and Dame Peggy Ashcroft.

Since coming to Denver in 1947, opera at Central City has occupied much of my life with time to see something like 187 performances up to 1992. The majority of these I have reviewed for local papers, including *The Denver Post* and the *Rocky Mountain News*, and such weeklies as *Cervi's Journal*, *City Edition*, *Straight Creek Journal*, *University Park News*, the *Sentinel* papers, *Rocky Mountain Journal*. Nationally I have reviewed productions at Central City for *Opera News, Musical America, Time* and *Variety*.

I am grateful to Polly Grimes, Nathaniel Merrill, Robert O'Hearn, John Moriarty, and the late Frank H. Ricketson, Jr. and Edwin Levy for their recollections and insights.

Most of all I am grateful for the patience and contributions to this volume of my wife, Barbara Young.

# DARING AND IMAGINATION

I first visited Central City in September 1936, on a drive with my family from Denver to Los Angeles. As we drove into the foothills of the Rocky Mountains, my mind was on some cherished reading, the current issue of *The American Mercury*, I believe. Other than noting the ruggedness of the steep canyon walls, I was making a strong case for juvenile boredom.

We made a tourist stop at Central City, the old mining town, where we walked about. I came to life when we found the opera house, pressing my eye to the keyhole to spy darkness. Posters advertising *The Gondoliers* were still up but that was the only sign of festive activity.

What kind of theater was this, in this seemingly desolate town? After the Festival was gone, what was left?

The ways people come to know Central City turn them either into lovers of the rickety, rackety old town, 8,000 feet high in the foothills, or into those so easily turned off by the haphazard streets with hordes of tourists going in and out of junky souvenir shops that their dislike becomes total.

Up one road is Culture, and down the others were the bars and the boisterous sounds of old-fashioned good times. Now the town has been engorged by a mania for machine-operated gambling which threatens the old rugged charm.

The idea of an opera house in a rude mining camp intrigued me, but it was not until 1947 that I would view a production at the Central City Opera House. Later I would come to know its impact on regional opera houses throughout the land. From Central City came ways of doing opera in America which originated there, and the tradition of singing in America as well came to thrive on styles of operatic presentations in that house.

From its founding in 1860, Central City developed a lusty theatrical tradition. Its first theater, the Montana, opened in the summer of 1862. Jack S. Langrische was the most popular of a steady stream of touring performers who played in Central City. His namesake, John Langrische, III, was on stage in the acting ensemble in 1932 when the theater was reopened. The original Langrische won the hearts of the Cornish, Irish, and Austrian populace with his light-hearted shenanigans.

In 1873 when the town had acquired a number of imposing brick structures President Grant paid a visit. The Presidential train left Denver at 8 in the morning for Golden where the party transferred to a train to Central City. Shortly after clearing Golden, the train broke down in Clear Creek Canyon, and awaited a substitute engine.

The President and party finally were delivered to Black Hawk at about 12:30 pm. Carriages transported the group to Central City, and the President emerged at the Teller House, the most imposing of the town's new buildings, walking to the entrance on a pavement of silver blocks valued at over $12,000, the town's special welcome.

The town had changed little from that described by poet Bayard Taylor after his 1866 visit, when he wrote: "The whole string of four cities has a curious rickety, temporary air, with their buildings standing as if on one leg, their big signs and little accommodations, the irregular wandering streets, and the bald, scarred and pitted mountains on either side."

In 1874 the town was nearly destroyed by fire but was quickly rebuilt, bricking itself up against further fire damage. In 1877 the Belvidere Theater on the site the fire station had earlier filled was built to last, and in fact was much in use until 1991 when it was rebuilt as a casino.

Two presentations of *The Bohemian Girl* at the Belvidere drew such a heavy crowd that the townspeople were convinced a genuine opera house was needed. A committee was formed, and $20,000 was raised for this construction. In March 1878 the Central City Opera House was opened.

It was designed by Robert S. Roeschlaub with gracefully arched doorways and a diminutive exterior balcony above the entrances. It is an attractive building which suggests the power of its four-foot-deep rock walls.

Many years later Richard R. Bretell in *Historic Denver: The Architect and Architecture, 1858-1893* aptly described the opera house:

"The Central City Opera House is indubitably Roeschlaub's best known building. Its austere stone facade gives the smallish building a sobriety and grandness lacking in most buildings of the Second Empire style. Probably for budgetary reasons, Roeschlaub eschewed the opportunity to cover the building in ornament. He divided the facade into three blocky masses, a central area with a mansard roof flanked by towers, and succeeded in giving the building a great deal more solidarity and depth than its neighboring street buildings with their implacably flat facades. The Central City Opera House is admirable for its straight-forwardness and simplicity. There is little waste, and the whole building has a lightness of execution typical of Roeschlaub's best buildings."

A very practical description of the theater appears in Harry Miner's American Dramatic History: "Horace M. Hale, manager. Seating capacity, 800. Rental, one night, $40; three nights, $100, share also, license included. Size of stage, 40 by 50 feet. Height of grooves from stage, 20 feet; height from stage to rigging loft, 40 feet. Depth under stage, 10 feet. Number of sets of scenery, 8. Leader of orchestra, Albert Lintz."

Travel to Central City from Denver was something of a problem for traveling troupes but they were not daunted. 17 touring companies played Central City during the 1881-82 season, whereas 20 played in the more easily accessible Georgetown's McClelland Hall, and 33 in Leadville's Tabor Opera House.

It was not much easier when the Central City Opera Festival was started up in the thirties. A headline in a June 1935 *Rocky Mountain News* proclaimed "Central City Easy to Reach," preceding a story which explained that access to Central City led over "Winding roads 60 miles from Denver to the little mining town."

However much vigor was in Central City's theater, mining was on the wane, with a gold strike in Cripple Creek taking many from Central City in the late 1880s.

The vision of big times in the mining towns was ending with the government ceasing its silver purchase policy after 1893. This hurt Central City whose economic base was entirely in mining activities.

In the late 1920s there was some mining when low, depression wages made it feasible. In the 1930s after the gold standard was ditched, the price of gold rose from $20 to $35 per fine ounce. In these times the town found tourism a dependable if periodic source of revenue after the revival of the opera house.

Nothing in Central City was more extraordinary than the opera house, which like Perrault's Sleeping Beauty was doomed to lie in obscurity until a show of affection restored it to life.

Many bestowed good wishes on the opera house, but undeniably its rescuers were two middle-aged women, Anne Evans and Ida Kruse McFarlane.

Anne Evans was the daughter of Colorado's first territorial governor, John Evans. Ida Kruse McFarlane was a professor of English at the University of Denver who married into the McFarlane family of Central City.

Since the very beginnings of the opera house the McFarlanes had been deeply involved in its fortunes. William and Peter had come to Central City as young men to work on its construction. William met his wife, Elizabeth, when she came from the East to visit her uncle, Horace M. Hale, the manager of the opera house.

The city had originally owned the building but it was later acquired by Senator H.R. Wolcott who subsequently sold it to Gilpin County which considered turning it into a courthouse. In 1882 it was purchased by the Gilpin County Opera House Association, at which time Horace Hale took it for a five-year lease.

Several years into the lease, Hale asked Peter McFarlane to manage the theater for him. He had lately discovered the structure to be severely threatened by timber and rock damage caused by the flooding of the creek that runs below as a constant threat.

In 1896 McFarlane installed electric lighting after beginning to buy up shares in the opera house so he could have entire control of its future. When Hale sold him his stock in 1900 for $900, McFarlane became its owner.

McFarlane immediately invested about $3,000 in roof repairs, wall refinishing and ceiling repairs, and also acquired hickory straight-backed chairs. He succeeded in getting voided a prohibition of Sunday performances, but was unable to shake the city fathers from prohibiting Sunday pre-performance parades, those events so crucial to interesting the townspeople in attending the theater.

Despite his endeavors to better the quality of touring companies, hard times made this difficult. In 1907 he lost $250, and after May 1908 was forced to close down the opera house. Occasionally the house would be opened up for school graduations, community events and political rallies. Once in a while a professional acting company would turn up, but mostly the theater was shuttered.

In 1910 a motion picture was shown in Central City in a crude store-front situation. This quickened interest in this new kind of entertainment. Rapidly, McFarlane went into the business of showing films in the opera house, opening July 4, 1910, but there were too few good films, and presently the novelty wore off, and there were losses.

By the twenties McFarlane diagnosed the Central City situation as follows: "15% of our people died, 10% are in mourning, 25% have moved away, 35% are penniless, 15% out of employment, leaving only 10% to support amusements."

On January 1, 1927 when McFarlane was 78, he closed the opera house. He remained in Central City to worry about its future until deteriorating health required a move to Denver where he died in May 1929.

The opera house was left to his descendants, Frederick, George, and Yetta McFarlane Schroeder. For a tax payment of $128, George McFarlane assumed the ownership, making the purchase final in 1931 with a payment of $337.87. By now the building was rotting in disuse with no apparent means of support.

Brother Frederick's wife was Ida Kruse, once County Superintendent of Gilpin County Schools, the county wherein Central City lay. She attended Vassar, following up her Bachelor of Arts degree with a Master's degree. As a student, she was drawn to the enriching theatrical ideas of Gordon Craig, going to Dublin's Abbey Theater for further theatrical studies.

In Denver she was active in the Denver Civic Theater, a local community group which utilized the Little Theater at the University of Denver where she taught English. Active in many cultural organizations, her paths regularly crossed those of Anne Evans.

Anne Evans, a daughter of Governor John Evans, was born in London while her parents were on a Grand Tour. When she was three the family returned to settle in Denver in the family home at 13th and Bannock streets. Later she attended schools in Berlin and Paris. Still later she studied at the Art Students League in New York, working on painting and drawing.

Accounts of these two ladies come from Polly Grimes, the first woman to be a member of the executive committee of the Central City Opera House Association, who before that served as secretary of the Board, and was active on the Board through the early 80s.

Polly describes Ida Kruse McFarlane as "fastidious and fashionable," whereas Anne Evans she thought "the exact opposite of Ida - she didn't care a hoot about the way she looked - she just dressed the way she wanted to."

Ida and Anne were good for each other. Ida was quick and full of ideas, and Anne complimented this with rare common sense. As a member of Colorado's Founding Family, she had a special status in Denver, which gave a special lustre to those projects she took on.

"She didn't have to suggest twice," was Anne Evans' comment when asked about Ida's proposal that she join the effort to revive the opera house. Her enthusiasm was boundless, her work untiring. Anne Evans had no large personal presumptions. In 1937 she said, " I never went into anything in my life on a pass until as co-manager of the Central City project I was given a pass to a New York theater. Did I feel important!"

She was learning how to put her name and her disposition to the benefit of things she considered important. "You have to get angry sometimes or they'll think they can run over you, especially if you are a woman," she once said. But Anne was a calming influence and sweetly reasonable. She was as pungent as she ever got in her famous exclamation to Ida in an early discussion when she asked, "How'll you get the people up there, Ida, by balloon?" Anne intended only to "stay with Central City until it got a leg up," she told friends.

Polly Grimes remembers Anne Evans as "a wonderful person to work with." When Polly drove Anna Kaskas, Orpheus of the 1941 *Orpheus* production, to Estes Park, a seventy mile drive, it took them much longer than planned. On their return the next day they ran into Anne Evans who had been made aware of their absence by worried producer Frank St. Leger. She asked them brightly, "Did you have a good time?"

Later in the Central City years word got around that the executive board and other members of the Association were personally profiteering from the Festival. Anne Evans led the planning for a luncheon at the Teller House for the Board of Gilpin County Commissioners, the Central City Council, and other concerned citizens. Disclosure and explanation of finances was the principal focus of this affair, and Anne Evans did not miss the opportunity to stress the evident need for continuing support from Central City and Denver, with as much as $60,000 needed to balance off the 1934 season.

Anne Evans developed a policy, a proposal that no limits existed on the kind of theater that could be done at Central City, "if it were done more beautifully than it has ever been done before."

Ida Kruse recognized the potential of the opera house for unique , artistic presentations, but her bent was language rather than theater. She did want the McFarlanes to have a clear title, and subsequently convinced them that the opera house should be donated to the University of Denver, or its legal description, Colorado Seminary. It was 1931 before this could be done.

In order for the University to acquire the property, a recommendation that it do so was needed. The trustees concluded the issue should be decided by the Board of the

Denver Civic Theater, which consisted of Anne Evans, Edna James Chappell, and Allen True, the painter.

Edna James Chappell had been on the Broadway stage, and her husband, Delos, was stagestruck as well as familiar with the fine arts. The Chappell family was prominent in Denver arts circles. Delos and his sister Jean (Mrs. George) Cranmer had presented the old family home at 13th and Logan Street to The Allied Arts where the Denver Art Association evolved into the Denver Art Museum. The American Native Arts Collection was housed there for a great many years.

By mid-May the trustees had made a positive recommendation, but there were infinite problems to be resolved before the opera house could start to function again.

In his annual address to the Board in 1956, Frank H. Ricketson, Jr., movie theater executive who was president of the Association from 1941 to 1965, gave his view of the origin of the idea of reviving the opera house.

"One beautiful spring day early in 1931, Ida - seeking professional endorsement of her idea - invited Walter Sinclair to drive to Idaho Springs, then go over the Virginia Canyon Road to Central City. Picnic lunches were packed, and Ida, Fred, and Walter Sinclair started on their way. Down muddy Floyd Hill they slid and plowed, and from rut to rut they struggled over the Virginia Canyon Mine Ore Trails into Central City.

"Before they had returned to Denver, Ida had the professional endorsement of Walter Sinclair. At the next informal meeting of the little group, an entirely new concept of a summer experimental theater with nationally recognized artists was born.

"A few weeks later - Ida, Anne Evans, Allen True, Delos and Edna Chappell made a heart-breaking, depressing inspection trip to Central City. They found that the opera house roof leaked, the foundation had suffered from erosion in its location over a stream bed, and the building in its present condition was unsafe for use. Any thought of a production in 1931 had to be abandoned. Anne Evans, serving as financial officer, began the first money-raising campaign for a project which still existed only in theory.

"The little group had taken the name of the Central City Opera House Committee, and their first recorded meeting was held in the offices of the Evans Investment Company in the Central Savings Building on December 10, 1931. Those present were Miss Anne Evans, Miss Anne Struthers, Mrs. Ida Kruse McFarlane, Mrs. Yetta McFarlane Schroeder, and Mrs. Ruth Brown Park. Another meeting took place a week later when artists Allen True and Paschal Quackenbush were present.

At this meeting, to squelch the doubters, a letter from Robert Edmond Jones was read in which he said that "only death or world cataclysm would prevent his being present and producing the opening performance."

At the start the usage of the opera house was vague. Walter Sinclair, the English born director of the Denver Civic Theater, so suave he was known as "Sir Walter," thought American melodrama of the 19th century would be perfectly at home there, and he envisaged a production of *East Lynne*. The trustees thought some kind of annual dramatic festival might be staged by the University of Denver Theater Department.

Some financial stability was provided when Anne Evans had the idea of selling to individuals, in honor of a family member or an historic personage, the old hickory chairs Peter McFarlane had acquired in 1900. Names and an appropriate date would be carved into the backs of these chairs, and these memorials went for $100 each. Some takers purchased three or four chairs, and all were sold. In current use, they are both admired for their historic resonance and cursed for their discomfort.

Allen True headed the renovation committee, restoring the murals himself. Denver architect Allan Fisher was called in for new designs for the rotting musicians' balcony above the entrance. The air within the house was so polluted the clean-up crew had to wear gas masks. Quackenbush, another Denver painter, assisted in the repainting and refurbishing so necessary. But soon the house again sparkled in its unique beauty.

If there had been vacillation about the use of the theater, it vanished with the arrival of Robert Edmond Jones. Just as the hand of fate seemed to bring Anne Evans and Ida Kruse McFarlane together in restoration of the opera house so that it might have a new life, so it seemed destiny had led Jones there as director and designer for six seasons.

Delos Chappell had known Jones in New York and shared the almost universal admiration for Jones's achievements with light and color in such imposing theatrical splendors as the John Barrymore *Hamlet*, O'Neill's *The Great God Brown*, and Marc Connolly's *The Green Pastures*. The Chappells worked on Jones and were able to attract his interest.

Jones was indeed the dean of American theatrical designers, and Chappell had struck what was a genuine coup in getting him to come to Central City. Jones focused his energies on bringing the best in spoken drama and the musical theater to its stage.

Jones would draw many fine talents to Central City - Lillian Gish, Walter Huston, Gladys Swarthout, Frank St. Leger - and the presence of artists of this caliber drew yet other creative people there. Although it was never easy to do things there, it was possible to become excited and inspired by what did get done. Success fed further success.

When Jones decided to do *Camille* by Alexander Dumas as the opening work in 1932 he cast Lillian Gish as the Lady of the Camellias. He was producer, director, and designer, and he saw to it that a strong cast was in support, with such actors as Ian Wolfe, Raymond Hackett, and Cora Witherspoon. The cast stayed at Heidi's Chalet beyond Black Hawk, with the women on one side of the resort hotel and the men on the other.

In her short history of the Central City Opera House, Edna James Chappell wrote, "When I wired Mr. Jones the whole story last summer and asked if he would be interested, he answered 'I should like to do a glamorous unheard-of-production of *The Lady of the Camellias* with a visiting star of the first magnitude,' and he is doing it."

"The ghosts had spoken to us," she continued," and we were bound, a little mystically we felt, to review their theater."

Jones approached his productions as though he had carte blanche, and for several years that was accepted. Florence Hemsley Burnet, close to the organization from the outset, wrote that "for five years or more Jones's contract states that he may produce anything he likes, in any way he desires, only it must be the best."

He told the artist Mabel Sibell Wolle, as she recounted years later, "I come to Central City with the idea of helping to create a vital new moment in the theater, not to make pretty little productions for summer vacation consumption."

Several years later Jones talked about *Camille*, calling it "an imperishable memory of beauty really truly enshrined in our hearts."

For *The New York Times* in June 1933 he wrote of the 1932 opening,"Indeed I shall never forget the glamour of the first night. The full moon rising over the bare hills to the east, the old barouches and phaetons (for modern motors were banned) drawn by white mules up the steep streets, the liveries footmen, the bustles and furbelows, the lace, the rubies and diamonds and emeralds, the audience of splendor - and on the stage the actors living out their brief magical hour, the 'big scenes' delicately underscored by music exquisitely rendered, the wild applause, the profusion of flowers that swept over the footlights, the rare Acadian atmosphere, the high delight that is so badly lacking, alas, on Broadway."

Frank Ricketson many years later remembered that *Camille* was "nearly played in the dark," the original lighting facilities at the opera house being so primitive. At first audiences were very small, and it would take many years of effort to turn attention to Central City on any substantial scale.

The newsmen who covered Central City's revival were delighted to have such a novelty to write about. Amidst the outpouring of adjectives they registered an enthusiasm for what was being termed an "American Salzburg." The wrongness of this reference missed awareness of the grand operas, stirring theater, the powerful orchestral base of the Vienna Philharmonic Orchestra, and the capacity to provide notable musical-theatrical experiences to over 5,000 people in one day.

World class performers are drawn to Salzburg by the magnetism of history, its Mozartean ambience, and audiences follow. Central City has a single facility which seats 756 plus other halls and churches of small capacity. The potential was being overstated.

Such individuals as Lucius Beebe, Hedda Hopper, and Ernie Pyle wrote much lively copy from Central City, but for every discerning and witty word there were hundreds attempting to evoke "the rollicking days of the gold rush."

Transportation was an ongoing headache but these crude operatic excursions were accepted by the majority with good humor. The Colorado and Southern Railway sent special trains up Clear Creek Canyon to Black Hawk, leaving Denver at 3 pm. Stagecoaches met the train to carry opera goers to Central City, a steep mile up the grade. Buses and excursion cars also were available.

On old U. S. 40 it was forty miles to Idaho Springs from Denver, and perilous Virginia Canyon lay ahead. Fortunately one-way driving was established prior to and after performances.

Though operatic activity in Central City was surprising, Jones had the name that could interest major talents in coming there. Among visitors in the opening season were Leopold Stokowski, George Jean Nathan, and Mable Dodge Luhan, and Central City was written up as an "in" place to be. Later, Rudolf Bing and Edward Johnson, the managers of the Metropolitan Opera, Lily Pons and Charles Laughton would be among its visitors.

It was reported that in the first season of one week, 94.6% of the seats were sold. Delos Chappell covered the 1932 deficit which was about $230,000.

For the 1933 *The Merry Widow* Jones was able to attract the beauteous operatic mezzo Gladys Swarthout to play Valencienne and Richard Bonelli, after Lawrence Tibbett the most admired baritone of the day. Natalie Hall, the then reigning queen of Broadway operetta, was The Widow. This time the Festival was extended to two weeks in mid-August.

One critic wrote that "Gladys Swarthout was not in excellent voice in the first act but her singing later was beautiful. The orchestra leader however drowned her low and mellow voice except in the upper register." *Time* was there to report typically that "No Rip Van Winkle apparition in the mountains, all this was Colorado's second Annual Play Festival blowing on the cold ashes of the onetime mining boomtown."

In a letter to the Executive Committee, Jones defined the quality of opera and theater as he saw it. " I do not want to bring," he wrote,"the established prima donnas - the Tetrazzinis or the Schumann-Heinks - who have a reputation but have had their day in the operatic world. I want to bring young singers who have gorgeous voices and who have their futures before them but who will look the part as well as act the part."

Despite the effort all was not perfection. On the closing night of *The Merry Widow*, stage hands, in closing night euphoria, jammed the garden door to the pavilion with a ball of twine so that it forced Frederick Warlock to improvise comedy for twenty minutes until he could get the door open.

It was during the run of *The Merry Widow* that Delos Chappell, so instrumental in getting Jones to Central City, began having second thoughts about him. He had always believed Jones capable of making the revival succeed on a high artistic level. After attending a *Merry Widow* rehearsal in which Jones talked and talked without actually rehearsing the company, Chappell began to feel that Jones was not delivering and must go.

His feelings about Jones were intensified as he worked hard with stage props. Chappell had volunteered his Rolls Royce for use in carrying small items of furniture and other properties from Denver to Central City, and on some days the car made as many as five trips. The more he worked the more he felt unappreciated, and adamant about Jones.

Chappell now urged that the Board reject a proposed five- year contract. Anne Evans wrote in support of Jones, and the executive committee asked that Chappell not attend further rehearsals.

In an effort to patch up the shattered relations, Edna James Chappell urged a meeting between Jones and Chappell but they both were disinclined. Chappell was wholly determined to put the screws on Jones.

In June of 1933 Jones had announced in The New York Times "Next year I intend to produce *Hamlet* and perhaps *Carmen*. And after that *Othello* and *Tristan* and *The Rosenkavalier*. Here I repeat is the most enchanting , the most glamorous theater in America, an old ever-new theater in our time."

There was no escaping the breadth of Jones's ambitions. Theatrically knowledgeable individuals such as Harold Clurman shared with Chappell some skepticism of his directorial method. Clurman describes in his *The Fervent Years* words Jones spoke to cast members of Stark Young's *The Saint* during a rehearsal Jones was directing.

"The theater is revelation. I look about me here, and I do not perceive drama. I do not feel revelation," after which Jones walked up the aisle and out of the theater. Clurman himself found the speech affecting but also thought "he made no connection with his actors. They could not be blamed for being embarrassed by his talk. They did not speak his language." Such concerns Chappell may well have shared.

The tone of activities at the opera house would change distinctly in 1934 when Jones produced *Othello*. He had hoped to do *Hamlet* with John Barrymore in a revival of the 1922 Broadway production. In these years Barrymore was making his best pictures, such as *Grand Hotel*, *Dinner at Eight*, and *Twentieth Century*, and although there always were line memory problems he found ways of performing with the aid of boards with dialogue written in large letters to prompt him.

Jones had been involved in preparing to film Barrymore in a color version of *Hamlet* which he would design and direct, but in December 1933 those old Barrymore memory problems recurred with intensity. *Hamlet*, on film or at Central City, would be out of the question.

Jones was fascinated by the film medium, and the following year the prospects of being active in Hollywood returned when he designed the settings and supervised the visual aspects of the first successful films in the new, improved three-color Technicolor process, the short *La Cucaracha*, and followed it with *Becky Sharp*, directed by Rouben Mamoulian.

When Barrymore was definitely out of *Hamlet*, Jones sought Fredric March of films but these overtures came to nothing because March was in greater demand in Hollywood than Barrymore. An announcement was made that *Hamlet* would be done on alternate nights with *Carmen*, and there is record of Edna James Chappell having wired Charlie Chaplin an invitation to appear as Hamlet.

In 1924 Walter Huston had starred in Jones's production of O'Neill's *Desire Under the Elms*. From 1929 through the early thirties Huston had concentrated on films but in the winter of 1933-34 he returned to Broadway in Sidney Howard's adaptation of Sinclair Lewis's *Dodsworth*. Huston interrupted this very successful production, said to be bringing in $30,000 a week, to come to Central City.

The Central City archives preserves Jones's telegram to Huston, a classic bit of correspondence. "Dear Walter," it read, "I would like to invite you and Nan (his wife, Nan Sunderland) to come out next summer to Central City, a little mining town in the mountains West of Denver, to do a production of Shakespeare's *Othello* for several weeks. I can offer you $1,000."

Huston wired back: "Dear Bobby, your terms are entirely unsatisfactory; I accept."

Ben Bezoff, who appeared in the *Othello* as Montano, and was a Denver radio personality and later director of Stapleton Airport, passed on collections of early days at Central City to me many years ago.

Bezoff recalled Jones's insistence that "velvet had to be velvet." He was determined to evoke a strong mood in the production through use of color, sound, and lighting. In one scene he used a great bell, and Kenneth McKenna who played Iago missed the swinging of the bell while shifting about on the stage, and ran into the downswing of the bell, which momentarily floored him. McKenna had acquired a look of great intensity about the eyes from having to appear tense as a dramatic actor. Members of the audience were overheard referring to "those burning eyes."

Bezoff recalls Huston as being "down to earth as doughnuts, just like an old shoe." He recalled that after performances the cast would gather in the Little Kingdom bar at the Teller House to hear him sing old vaudeville ditties. Huston always had a good word for the young actors, "valiant hopefuls," he called them, much touched by their theatrical talents. He encouraged them in their eagerness to "carry their own dreams on to the world."

There are other recollections of Central City by Polly Grimes. She recalls how delightfully relaxed were activities around the opera house before the town became overcrowded, when singers would relax on the old railroad benches by the opera house after rehearsals, and would go on picnics, sunbathe, and cool off in the streams.

Social life expanded when Mr. and Mrs. Spencer Penrose of Colorado Springs fortunes became intrigued by Central City. He would load his limousine with champagne, and invited singers and Board members to their Central City home to share the bubbly atmosphere. And there were other evenings when singers would let their hair down and play and sing in the McFarlane house.

There were still other sociable occasions in the Eureka Ballroom at the Teller House where a night club was set up for such popular New York entertainers as Sheila Barrett, Tamara, John Buckmaster, and the magician, Russell Swann to perform their sophisticated routines.

The Penroses brought more than champagne to Central City. Between 1933 and 1956 Mrs. Penrose gave over $400,000 to the Association. In 1947 she financed the construction of the additional exit from the balcony into the upper garden, as well as the fastening together of the old hickory chairs in the parquet and dress circle. There were also improved dressing rooms, modernization of stage facilities, miscellaneous construction and shop work.

While there was a desire for high quality amusement, Jones did point out to the executive committee that he did "agree throughly with all objectors, that there is a certain risk in producing anything in Central City that is not of the nature of light and summer fare, they should at the same time remember that our aim is for a higher and grander one than this."

Frank Ricketson, who had been a spectator at the Jones-Chappell dispute, was aware that Jones had one problem-provoking habit: he would take three hours for his morning coffee. But Jones used to come to Ricketson and cry on his shoulder, telling him," I'm going to go to Tombstone, Arizona where there are no dramatic critics."

Many writers expressed to Edna James Chappell their interest in writing plays expressly for the opera house stage. Robert Frost wrote to her, "I'll try to write one for it when I know the country better." Dan Totheroh wrote that he would like to write for Helen Hayes a play about Lotta Crabtree, the child actress who portrayed young girls into her middle age, and then retired to her home at Grass Valley, California.

For 1935 the dramatic pickings were slim. At one time there was a notion of doing a play called *Growing Pains* with the youthful film players Anne Shirley and Junior Durkin, but then Jones conceived of that something different towards which he was always impelled, a musical review, *Central City Nights*.

This was to be an evening of olios such as would have been popular in Central City's hey-day. No one seems to have mentioned that in those early days the musical interludes came between acts of a five-act melodrama. But it was going to be a pleasant exercise in nostalgia as Jones saw it. What music would not be drawn from the old popular songs was written by Waldo Williamson of Denver. Frank St. Leger came to conduct, while Jones indulged himself in the fol-de-rol atmosphere of early Central City.

This was the first of eleven seasons, continuing up to 1952, in which St. Leger was to be involved at Central City as an influence bringing strength to musical aspects there.

His musical knowledge and rigorous application of his ideals, coupled with theatrical sensitivity, made him a significant element of whatever his particular responsibilities were for a particular season. When after the war he became producer of an expanded Festival, he acquired an authority comparable to that of Jones in the early years.

In 1922 a very young St. Leger had come to Denver with the distinguished Freida Hempel and the tenor Edward Johnson to accompany them in a musical program at the opening of radio station KLZ.

St. Leger was born of Australian parents in Madras, India. As a young conservatory graduate he was accompanist to Dame Nellie Melba. Before going to the Metropolitan Opera in 1939 he led the Chicago Civic Opera, the American Opera Company, and the Houston Symphony. He combined artistry and practical business matters with an ideal balance.

One of the featured players in *Central City Nights* was the lovely young Josephine Neri, who many years later recalled to me how touched she was when just before each performance Jones presented her with a single, fresh rose. She also remembered Central City as so rainy and muddy that to get up the hillsides to her rooms it was necessary to use ropes. Later steps were built for shortcuts.

Jones had difficulties keeping things on the high professional basis he preferred. During Nan Sunderland's dramatic tomb scene from Shakespeare's *Antony and Cleopatra* someone flushed a dressing room toilet, an intrusion which caused actresses Mary Porter and Helen Freeman, doing the scene with Sunderland, to shake with uncontrollable laughter.

St. Leger had written a dirge for them to sing during this scene, and its difficulties got them off to a bad start at one performance. They were aware that this would earn a reprimand from St. Leger so they left the theater directly after the performance without stopping to remove their makeup, and they ran right into St. Leger who was just as aroused as they anticipated.

Jones's influence on the Central City Festival was not universally admired. The *Rocky Mountain News* in editorials and in columns reflected this attitude. Lee Casey, a *News* columnist, wrote in one of his columns of the "artsy-smart boys" as he expressed his belief that the Association should stage a drama about life in a mining camp by a Colorado playwright.

It has been no secret, the *News* editorialized, "that some members (of the Board) look with disfavor on the long tenure of Jones as director, believing a change of influence would be good for the annual play in the mountain mining town, which has become famous as a shrine of the theater." In March 1936 the *News* seemed to crow with the word that "Central City Loses Jones as Director."

Jones had continued to spend time in Hollywood but since *Becky Sharp* he had done nothing. He would have liked to have been a major influence but his apparent lack of the required commercial attitude prevented further involvement there, and fortunately for the stage he dismissed film as a passing fancy.

It was St. Leger who produced the 1936 offering, *The Gondoliers* by Gilbert and Sullivan, the first of many G & S triumphs there. Paul Porter directed the show which attained considerable popularity, and St. Leger conducted.

Neither Jones nor St. Leger figured in the 1937 production of Ibsen's *A Doll's House*, done in a new version by Thornton Wilder, directed by Jed Harris, with settings by Donald Oenslager who would design for this stage more than any other designer. The illustrious acting company was headed by Ruth Gordon with Walter Slezak, Dennis King, and Sam Jaffe.

With few cast changes this production went on the road from Central City, and when it arrived in New York it played eighteen weeks on Broadway where Alexander Woolcott loudly sang its praises over his national radio program. It was widely known in New York that the production originated in Central City.

For the 1937 season Richard Aldrich had served as producer, and he would return in 1938 and 1939 as Associate Producer, in 1938 with Jones to do *Ruy Blas*, and in 1939 with St. Leger to do *Yeoman of the Guard*.

*Ruy Blas* was said to have been chosen out of obscurity by Jones to "keep the Festival from getting in a rut." Bramwell Fletcher and Helen Chandler of stage and screen were the featured performers, along with Percy Waram and Nance O'Neil, in this Brian Hooker adaptation of Victor Hugo's drama. There was music by Waldo Williamson.

Jones had more to say about programming for Central City. "People wonder why we don't select frothy musical comedy or light opera for the Central City Festival. It is because going back to the days when the pioneers built the opera house, they paid generously and worked hard to produce the big things of the theater for its stage. Their order was in effect, 'Give us the best.' The best then, as now, is found in the great romances."

In 1939 it was a return to Gilbert and Sullivan with *The Yeoman of the Guard*, produced by Frank St. Leger, who also conducted. Felix Brentano, admired by Virgil Thomson for his work with the New Opera Company in New York City, was stage director. Charles Kullman, Anna Kaskas, and Hilda Burke from The Met, Natalie Hall and Richard Hale from operetta filled out a cast of abundant talent. It was claimed that in its run this production was attended by more than 14,000 persons.

More and more newcomers were settling into Central City, acquiring houses, upgrading them, and carrying on an enviable social life. Ida Kruse and Fred McFarlane were among those whose Central City nights were made more alive by the visiting celebrities with their singing and impersonations.

In later years Lucius Beebe became a regular. He seemed invariably delighted with the productions which he described in rapturous detail for *The New York-Herald Tribune*. He would arrive in Denver on his private railroad car prior to the opening, sweep up to Central City where his numerous friends hosted him after the opening, and he would depart the following day.

He was famous for being reluctant to travel the winding Virginia Canyon Road. His preferred traversal was on the floor of a car with a bottle in hand, sipping his way into oblivion. It was out of sight, out of mind, and if he could not see the curves and worry about precipitous drops, he took away a more favorable impression of his visit.

Ruth Gordon also was terrified of the winding dirt road, and once denied herself a party at Eleanore Weckbaugh's over worry about the trip.

These parties at the palatial Weckbaugh French chateau overlooking Denver Country Club were said by some to be command performances for the performers, but at these Monday affairs when the singers took a day off, the liquor flowed freely, there was swimming in the pool, ample food, and many celebrity hungry Board members came to acknowledge this perquisite.

Her parties were celebrated in verse by friends who sang,
"Ellie, Ellie, we've been thinking
When we all are far away,
Of the cool of the pool,
And we'd like to stay and play."

Attention to society activities at Central City in the Denver dailies almost drove the actual Festival out of the papers. How the Denver society leaders were gowned, and who was with whom seemed to exceed the attention given the actual productions in the value systems of the local editors.

Anne Evans must have been appalled by the description of herself at one opening, "in black lace combined with chiffon, with diamond clips distinguishing the neck line." In 1933 *Vogue* reported on the 1932 grand opening - "the oldest Denver aristocracy came dressed in the original costumes of the period of the theater's opening. In Paquin, Worth, and Doucet creations covered with family jewels . . they braved peril and nosebleed and discomfiture in that high wilderness."

It was apparent the existence of the Festivals depended upon the largesse of Denver society. Central City had become an exclusive playground for the wealthy who had an interest in the arts. They thus made it possible for the less affluent to enjoy fresh operatic productions and distinctive theater when these were not available in Denver.

The concern for the theater in opera which marked opera at Central City in the forties was matched in America by San Francisco alone, for production standards at The Met were delinquent in this aspect of its operatic productions.

Very early it was decided that opera at Central City would be done in English, a tradition that has been maintained since opera first took its stage. To its credit, this decision was one of the things that made opera in Central City an intimate experience. A flaw in doing opera in English is that the majority of translated librettos totally miss the wit and poignancy and poetry of the original, and frequently destroy musical values.

The expert promoter of these Central City efforts was the bright young man-about-town, Kansas-born eager beaver, Frank H. Ricketson, Jr. With his friend, Charles Yeager, he created "Bank Night" during depression times in the midwest, a "bonanza" he would later recall. He managed National Theaters into becoming the major motion picture theater chain of the mountain states, Fox-Intermountain Theaters.

Initially Rick was errand boy for Anne Evans, as he described his earliest function within the Central City organization. Whatever tests she was putting him to, he passed well.

His first efforts on behalf of Central City were to make fund-raising visits with Anne Evans to prominent Denver businessmen. He was struck by her hard-headedness and determination, and recalls her as "one of the smartest women I'd ever met."

If they were turned down, she would advise him, "Don't be impatient." Or of one man she would say, "He just hasn't learned how to give." This particular individual eventually capitulated to the impressive lady's requests, and within months was opening his check book as the two walked into his office, saying, "How much do you want?"

Anne Evans always "wished things to be in color," Ricketson has remembered. Gambling in Central City was one of its most colorful aspects until the slot machines and other accepted games were eliminated in 1949.

Anne Evans did not support gambling but she thought it should be retained in Central City as a reminder of early days. The Denver gambling interests had taken over the responsibility of protecting Central City against infighting by other illicit interests. Anne Evans was put in touch with O.E. "Smiling Charlie" Stephens who arranged a meeting with Mike Mongone from Leadville, kingpin of mountain gambling interests.

Miss Evans, Stephens, and Rick were driven to Central City in Stephens's limousine, Rick going along to uphold Anne Evans and the Association. At the Teller House they met Mongone to whom Stephens made introductions, saying "take care of this little lady." And so for a while slot machines continued to be available at the Teller House until in 1949 the Colorado general assembly made them illegal. But in 1992 gambling returned in hurricane force to Black Hawk and Central City.

Jones was elsewhere in 1940 when Smetana's *The Bartered Bride* was produced and conducted by St. Leger with Felix Brentano again serving as stage director. This was arguably the first opera to be done in the opera house, since *The Merry Widow* with its spoken dialogue is properly operetta.

The only darkening over Central City in 1940 was that Ida Kruse McFarlane, that "prim, sweet, and thoughtful person, a lady to the core," as Rick fondly recalled her, died on June 18, just three weeks before *The Bartered Bride* was to open.

A singularly large contingent came from The Met. The Marie was a darling at The Met, a Colorado native, Josephine Antoine, who was born in Denver, raised in Boulder, and had gone to Europe to study with the great Sembrich. Others were tenor John Carter, bass Normon Cordon, Louis D'Angelo, Met company member since 1917, and his daughter Louise, plus Helen Olheim, Thelma Votipka, and George Rasely, all esteemed artists.

Many hailed this offering, among them Thomas Hornsby Ferril, who wrote "On the credit side of the ledger, it never deviated from solid showmanship." In the *Rocky Mountain News,* Anne Stein Roth wrote that "The production has esprit, spritely good humor, and whistleable tunes, moreover the tempo is fast, and the comic situations sharply etched."

It now was getting easier to reach Central City. In July 1940, presidential candidate Wendell Willkie took time to come with Governor Ralph Carr. Carr met Willkie at 4:20 pm at Stapleton Airport, and they drove to Central City via the Mount Vernon Canyon Road, still visible from I-70. They took the then new road along Clear Creek to where the Creek turns East, and through the canyon to Black Hawk and up to Central City, arriving there about 6:30 for dinner preceding *The Bartered Bride*. But not everyone had a motorcycle escort. And no longer did the harrowing curves of Virginia Canyon need to be challenged.

For *The Bartered Bride*, whose infectious high spirits and colorful atmosphere were so successfully realized, there was also financial success, with a record-breaking attendance of 20,250 for its 24 performances. This extension into the three-week run proved an important scheduling change.

On January 6, 1941, not quite six months following the death of Ida Kruse McFarlane, Anne Evans was dead of a heart attack. Their passing, in combination with turbulent war years which in the end made opera temporarily impossible at Central City, indeed brought a new challenge for the next generation.

The old guard had delivered the guidance over to younger but well-schooled hands.

An executive committee consisting of Ricketson, Polly Grimes, Malcolm Wyer, Denver city librarian, and Milton Bernet, Association publicist, was named to supervise the 1941 Festival following the loss of the founders.

In 1941 the Festival arrived at a kind of artistic pinnacle, a time in which its forces were reckoned to be strong enough to present two operas in repertory over a three-week period. Rossini's *The Barber of Seville* and Gluck's *Orpheus and Euridice*, shortened to *Orpheus*, were offered with another large Met delegation on hand.

Jones returned to design both productions, St. Leger conducted, and the two were harmonious co-producers with Herbert Graf in his first Central City work as stage director.

The polished John Brownlee, who would return in 1965 to stage three operas, was the admired Figaro, with Stella Andreva, John Carter, and Louis D'Angelo as Rossini principals. The Gluck cast included Anna Kaskas as Orpheus, Margit Bokor, the Euridice of Bruno Walter's 1936 Salzburg production, filling that role, and Patricia Dunn sang Amor.

An increasingly important aspect of Central City opera productions would be its chorus, which served as a springboard into prominence for superior talents. For nine seasons the chorus was under the direction of Mrs. Florence Lamont Hinman, founder of the Lamont School of Music at the University of Denver, who seemed to define the word dowager. She was crusty but led with authority and was devoted to her young singers.

In the *News*, Anne Stein Roth acclaimed the *Orpheus* as "by far the most inspirational of any production of its kind ever to be given in the historic theater, *Orpheus* will long remain in the memories of local opera-goers." Frances Wayne of *The Denver Post* claimed to recognize an aria from Gluck's *Alceste* as an interpolation she did not believe to be warranted.

Everyone seemed to have an *Orpheus* story. Rick found a Texas Cadillac dealer on his hands on the Sunday of the opening. Wishing to attend the performance he persuaded the Texan to join him. Awash in the beauty of the production, the Texan declared the work was "the most beautiful thing I've ever seen."

It fell to Polly Grimes to escort Edward Johnson, the noted onetime tenor and at that time General Manager of the Metropolitan Opera, to *Orpheus*, and she chanced to see him wipe tears from his eyes during the performance.

Jones relished his return for so spectacular a season. In May 1941 he had told the *Rocky Mountain News* that "while other theaters may be more elaborate and pretentious, the Central City Opera House is truly the most beautiful in the country if not in the world."

After that summer's opening he was quoted in *Time*, "We're bringing great art here. Our grandfathers did. We hope you like it." In its inimitable manner, *Time* went on to review the *Orpheus* as "Lofty and noble was *Orpheus*, but not too much so." St. Leger also was quoted by *Time* in reference to the English adaptation, "We got the god-damned twaddle out of it."

The press was fond of Central City coverage. Ernie Pyle of the Scripps-Howard chain came in 1941 and devoted seven columns to the town atmosphere and the opera.

Denver journalists were not too jaded to write about Central City. Tom Ferril, the poet and publicist, observed that "It can be said of the theater of Central City as of probably no other commercial theater in America that its worst faults arise from the pursuit of excellence for its own sake."

Jones worked hard in his push for perfection at Central City, and increasing audiences and support for ambitious projects were starting to pay off. If before the 1941 season he had told *The Denver Post* that "the American people must acquire the Central City habit," it was as if he had been heard on a broad scale.

Ernie Pyle acclaimed what he had seen, writing, "I think the Festival's opening night comes close to being the country's No. 1 fantastic event."

Lee Casey grumbled over Central City's operatic aspirations, "Central City is getting out of hand - unless something is done to stop him, I can forsee Mr. St. Leger producing *La Boheme* next year and *Aida* in 1948." Only his notion of the timing would be wrong by a few years."

Casey missed the point of the Festival; he went on to write "That would mean that Central City would simply duplicate the productions of Monsignor Bosetti during the Denver opera season. Performances at Central City should be distinctive like Central City itself - should not necessarily be of Western origin but certainly should offer the playgoer something unusual, something not offered by New York or by the few companies that take to the road."

Casey urged good theater, and gave it some thought, then wrote, "Let us have *L'Aiglon* played by a man. How about having a big young actor, say Alan Ladd, to play the duke?"

Later in 1941 Ricketson took on the presidency which he held until 1964 when he became Chairman of the Board. Still later he became Honorary Chairman and then Chairman Emeritus. As a man of theater who drew no lines between stage and film, Rick was very much aware of the need to focus on worthy product, and of the many colorful ways to draw attention to Central City.

During his many years there would be a steady increase in support and attendance and attention to the Central City Opera House Association finances. As he once told a *News* reporter, "Never spend a dollar without knowing where it will come from."

The coming of the war and rationing of gasoline and rubber tires made cancellation of the 1942 Festival inevitable. The Association hated to let the Festival go, and went so far in its negotiations as to sign St. Leger to do *The Tales of Hoffman* but in early May it was canceled. There is no record of any thought to move the Festival to Denver for the duration. In those days the Festival could only be thought of in terms of productions at the venerable opera house.

In July 1945 Robert Edmond Jones was joined on the stage of the opera house by Josephine Antoine and Anna Kaskas for a broadcast to the nation, anticipating a second revival at Central City.

And on November 11, 1945 in the pages of *The New York Herald-Tribune*, Lucius Beebe announced the resumption of the Central City Opera Festival in 1946.

It would be a new chapter, to be written by men and women committed to the highest standards, bearing a tradition that had brought a memorable illumination to the dark years of depression.

Now the professionals would take over. Could they match the work of the rank amateurs who had put the opera house on the nation's artistic map?

# THE RICKETSON YEARS

A happy festivity marked the return of opera to Central City in 1946. There was every reason to think the renewal would advance the organization and its productions towards higher professional standards which in turn would kindle larger audiences and financial returns. In that zeal for professionalism lay the danger that Central City might lose the fresh spirit of innovation that had marked its first decade.

For Frank Ricketson it was a time of testing, and he was anxious to get on with the work of overseeing productions which so tantalized his theatrical leanings. He did not yet have a professional opera person's insight but he had seen to it that there was strength throughout the production team.

As a one-man support team for Anne Evans, he had gone with her on fund-raising calls, and learned where the money was. He had learned about artistic temperaments from Robert Edmond Jones himself, and knowing the value of such individuals, had learned patience. He was a professional theater manager on a large scale, and although the opera house was not to be compared with the forty or so film theaters operated by Fox-Intermountain Theaters, the aim was the same: to make them profitable through worthy product and astute management.

Rick was imposing in appearance, tall and an expert at working crowds and Board members and was hardly the artsy type Lee Casey loved to castigate. He exuded optimism and at the same time was a shrewd operator. It was not out of a void that he created Bank Night with its free dishware. He knew how to dish good feelings.

Jones was no amateur, nor was St. Leger, nor were Lillian Gish or Walter Huston, but at Central City they were joined in creating theater on an inventive, original level. And Rick was determined that the new beginning would continue the best of what had been done. Rick aimed to build on that tradition set by Anne Evans, and to make it work in a more efficient, modern manner.

Two operas were to be done in 1946, Mozart's *The Abduction From the Seraglio*, Central City's first Mozart, and *La Traviata*, which tipped its hat to that 1932 *Camille* which opened the house after its long closure.

It seemed strange that Robert Edmond Jones was not involved in this auspicious reopening but he was designing Eugene O'Neill's *The Ice Man Cometh*, and had removed himself physically as well as emotionally from Central City.

Jones had written years earlier of actors "that in the end they put aside the make-up and the vesture and go away into the darkness, leaving us only a few fading photographs and playbills and their imperishable memories." Jones himself though gone left a charge to the Association to work for perfection, and within the limits of the opera house and budgetary considerations, this was well observed by Rick.

It was Frank St. Leger who would provide continuity of artistic leadership. Rick recognized his efficiency as manager.He had conducted six productions at Central City, but it was a mark of his ambitions for the opera house that he chose not to conduct but to oversee as producer the work of Met conductor Emil Cooper and director Herbert Graf. The major talents of this threesome were to set high standards for three festivals, 1946-47-48.

Emil Cooper had won from critic Virgil Thomson the comment that he was "the only conductor on the Metropolitan's present staff," which then included Bruno Walter, George Szell, and Fritz Busch,"for whom the orchestra plays invariably in tune."

Among all those who staged opera, Herbert Graf had the highest ranking. At Salzburg, The Met, and San Francisco he had taken the idea of opera as theater and made gripping performances. It was a coup to have him come to Central City.

The Met had planned to feature the brilliant young soprano Eleanor Steber in a new production of Mozart's *The Abduction from the Seraglio*, at that time a rarity, and although no formal arrangement existed, the Central City production was clearly a trial effort to see just how it would play.

Cooper conducted and Graf directed both Central City and Met productions, with Eleanor Steber, John Carter, and Felix Knight singing in both *Abductions*. What The Met missed, and what was one of the brightest features of the Central City production was the Osmin of Jerome Hines, at 24 thought to be too young in experience for The Met stage. He stole the Central City show with his resonant bass and his movie star good looks.

The area critics chimed in enthusiastically. In *The Denver Post*, Alex Murphree described this *Abduction* as "a silver waterfall of charm . . . a brilliant pattern of theatrical delight." For Anne Stein Roth of the *News*, "The real star of the show is 24-year-old Jerome Hines." Settings by Donald Oenslager contributed richly to theatrical pleasures.

The Denver singer Frank Dinhaupt, a student of Florence Lamont Hinman at the Lamont School of Music, had changed his name to Francesco Valentino when he went to The Met in 1940. In his Central City debut he sang the elder Germont, a Denver boy making good. In 1935 for the Denver Grand Opera he had done his first elder Germont, and after a large ovation for his "Di Provenza il mar" aria, took a bow and proceeded to sing the Prologue from I *Pagliacci* as an encore. Such goings on were not approved at Central City.

Just as the 1941 *Orpheus* had been treasured, the *Traviata* is recalled with special affection, hailed at the time by William Hawkins of *New York World Telegram*, who remembered a deep blue Paris sky and a "startling yellow table." Oenslager's settings were done in varying shades of green, framing the tragic story of the Lady of the Camellias, told this time to Verdi's music.

The productions showed the Festival to be in sure hands. St. Leger was so deeply concerned with the quality and size of the orchestra that he wanted to enlarge the orchestra pit. This was a continuation of a struggle St. Leger had taken on in 1941, when after one of his outbreaks Robert Edmond Jones drew a sketch of the opera house interior in which the entire floor of the opera house was filled with musicians; the title of the drawing was "Mr. St. Leger makes his last enlargement of the orchestra."

The new president, Ricketson, began to develop a broad, progressive outlook. In January 1947 he gave the first of his many informative annual addresses as President, saying "always we must strive to plan to surpass our previous efforts. The day that Central City compromises for one moment with inferior quality, the day we forsake for an instant the great art of the stage, whether opera or drama, the day that Central City becomes a carnival midway in a dusty ghost town, then Colorado will have lost its distinctive memorial to its pioneers.

"Our two productions last year (1946) cost approximately $100,000, and our box office was $66,000. The $34,000 difference between our expenses and our receipts retained for us the title of 'the summer theater capital of America' and brought recognition to our state which couldn't have been achieved in any other way for twenty times that sum. Our finance committee is starting a subscription fund of $35,000 this year because we want to hold recognition that is now ours."

With plans to do Beethoven's *Fidelio* in 1947, the indications were that this would be a banner year. *Fidelio*, Beethoven's only opera, demanding big voices, dramatic authority, and striking visual elements, would test the organization as nothing previously. Though the alternating Von Flotow *Martha* asked little, it would require elegance in its style.

The production team was on top of the serious demands. Although the guard had been changed and many younger people had come onto the board, Ricketson provided vigorous leadership.

Of theatrical designers, none was more sought after by opera and theatrical producers than Donald Oenslager. He was capable of high style, great dramatic breadth, and startling originality. When his vision was right he could design stunning sets. At other times, when his designing load became too heavy the results were too elaborate or rigid.

Frank St. Leger was able to stand apart from stage and pit activities to demand high standards. He took his responsibilities very seriously.

There was a strong team of vocal coaches, with Karl Kritz, a Met staff conductor, and Leo Muller. Kritz's wife, the singer Marguerite Piazza, was visiting him in Central City when Frances Greer, the Lady Harriet of *Martha*, lost her voice, so the vacationing Piazza tucked the score in a flower basket and behind a fan, with Met diva Lucrezia Bori in the audience for this particular matinee.

In a crisis at The Met, Regina Resnick substituted for an ailing Zinka Milanov in *Il Trovatore* in March 1945. Later, with Bruno Walter conducting, she sang Leonore in the first *Fidelio* done at the Met since Kirsten Flagstad's pre-war performances. By 1947 Resnick was a matured singer, esteemed critically at The Met. At Central City she had a brilliant success as Leonore.

The Florestan was Brian Sullivan, Sam in Kurt Weill's ground-breaking operatic *Street Scene* on Broadway. Kenneth Schoen was a veteran of the 1944 Met *Fidelio*, and he came to Central City as Pizzaro. Leslie Chabay sang Jacquino, with the charming Lois Hunt singing Marcellina. Another repeat from The Met was Lorenzo Alvary as Rocco. Florence Lamont Hinman prepared the chorus with special fervor.

I still recall vividly the excitement of *Fidelio*, my first opera at Central City, the dramatic power of the music, the eloquent singing, the staging, the cohesion and uniformity of execution. It was enthralling musical theater, superbly executed.

Since this first Festival in 1947 I have missed hearing but two operas in 45 years. I was unable to attend *Martha* in 1947 or *The Tales of Hoffman* in 1948.

A new precedent was set in 1947 with the presentation of *Harvey* by Denver's Mary Coyle Chase, following the opera for four weeks in August. Frank Fay of the Broadway Pulitzer Prize-winning production helped set a house record of $94,631 for its run, surpassed only in 1949 by Mae West's Diamond Lil which took in $95,872.

In those days, a loss of $7,646.80, for instance, was not hard to make up, but with Louis Calhern in the sophisticated *The Play's The Thing* in 1948, a loss of $12,777.70 was more to be noticed.

Ricketson touched on a number of intriguing topics in his President's address of November 10, 1947. He compared the growth of the Association, noticing the 1932 gross of $13,000 in a one week run, then noted the gross for the 1947 seven-week Festival was $167,149.

Rick recommended employment of a full-time business manager, that the Festival be extended to six weeks, to include three weeks of opera and three weeks of a play, and proposed establishment of a $25,000 donor's fund.

By 1948, Rick's vision of the Donor's Fund had grown to $35,000, and he realized that a reorganization of the committee structure was needed. To this end he sought out new Board members, members who could strengthen the financial picture.

Rick also wanted to have Critiques, as he chose to call them, symposiums bringing together specialists in opera and theater. He thought two afternoons of small symphony or chamber music should be included, and urged furthering of such social activities as a University of Denver Night, expansion of opening night festivities, an Opera Ball, a Miner's Jubilee, and free noon-day organ recitals.

The Critiques had started in 1947 with Burns Mantle and Hedda Hopper, and in 1948 Gypsy Rose Lee took part, along with critic-composer Virgil Thomson. In 1949 James Michener and Hanya Holm took part, and in what would be its final year, there were Dorothy Kirsten, Gaetano Merola, founder and director of the San Francisco Opera, and critic Olin Downes. These events had been well attended but no longer did it seem crucial for Central City to sponsor such gatherings.

At these events, good talk rather than high profundity was heard. Dorothy Kirsten told the audience a requisite of popular opera should be "that tenors should not eat so much spaghetti," while Downes thought "God was careless about where he distributed voices." Alex Murphree of the *Post* observed that opera was bound to be "unsatisfactory unless it is satisfying in all its parts."

By now it was becoming easier to reach the mountain town. Roads were so improved the forty-mile trip could be made in an hour and a half. Many, like *The New York Times's* Howard Taubman, were finding their way there from distant places. Taubman pointed out that Central City "was worth any American's attention. It is creating something fresh in a setting rich with color and history. If its standards are maintained, more and more tourists in the years to come will be heading towards Colorado for the music as well as the mountains."

Writing in the *Times* of the 1948 productions of *Cosi Fan Tutte* and *The Tales of Hoffman*, Taubman observed that "Donald Oenslager had accomplished a minor miracle in giving them (the operas) depth, variety and imagination" and found it news that "they were played with credibility."

This time the cast was less a consignment from The Met than a national gathering of young singers of promise. Jerome Hines, who had walked away with the 1946 *Abduction*, commanded attention as the villainous Dr. Copelius and Dr. Miracle. Others from the Met were Marilyn Cotlow, 1948 winner of the Metropolitan auditions, and Lorenzo Alvary who was to sing 983 performances at The Met over a thirty-year period.

The *Cosi* was engagingly chic, relishing the high sheen of the then novel celophane and plastics, and Oenslager took dazzling opportunity to exploit it. The Fiordiligi of the lovely Anne Bollinger swept across the stage like a charming zephyr. Her early death in the 50s while a member of the Hamburg Opera was indeed a tragic loss.

Limited in the number of dressing rooms, it had been necessary to erect tents but a Penrose gift made it possible to build an annex with dressing rooms and a costume shop to ease this problem.

Emil Cooper and Herbert Graf both were back in fine fettle, with St. Leger producing, and doing his expert balancing act.

Taubman did not hedge his opinions. He called *Cosi* "a production that any opera house might well be proud of. Its outstanding characteristic is its unity and cohesiveness. It is all of a piece musically, scenically, and dramatically. The whole thing has been put together with the care and taste possible under Festival conditions. That is the only way to do Mozart, for his operatic works flourish best when mounted with inclusive artistic imagination."

Virgil Thomson was one with a special appreciation of the opera house. In *The New York Herald-Tribune* he wrote of this Festival that the opera house had an "acoustical liveness, a fullness of resonance without any echo that is not equalled by more than a half dozen houses of its kind in the world. It is completely advantageous to music, makes everything sound bright and warm.

"That the performances were worthy of their enhancement," Thomson continued," is due to the producer, Frank St. Leger, and to the chief conductor, Emil Cooper . . . For general musical excellence, the performances were the equal of any opera performances available anywhere today, and far, far better than many produced in more pretentious circumstances."

Cecil Smith reviewed the productions for *The New Republic*, noting that they were done "with a liveliness and finish that put the Metropolitan among the also-rans." Smith went on to observe that "Oenslager's designs were bright and witty, if a bit too full of glittering celophane, and Graf, whose career had been damaged by the slip-shod way the Metropolitan gets things onto the stage, had ample rehearsals to demonstrate the brilliance of his directorial talent, and the deftness with which he can handle eighteenth-century comedy. The young cast had learned to sing the music with both zest and taste . . . Emil Cooper, the conductor, recaptured a vitality and enthusiasm he has lost at the Metropolitan."

At Central City, St. Leger was giving an exemplary display of what it means to produce opera. He could stand apart and see that there was an artistic cohesion. At the Met, he had been given the title of Executive Secretary, and he was regarded as an effective trouble-shooter. During the winter it was announced that for 1949 he would "act as overseer with the actual Central City productions charged to Dr. Elemer Nagy. "In both 1949 and 1950 programs St. Leger was given credit for "arrangements."

The years in which St. Leger had production responsibility were outstanding. Working closely with Rick, no financial problems marked them, and it seemed they had gone by much too swiftly in their completely professional way. Though it was not immediately noticed, he would be missed.

# THE HUNGARIAN

Elemer Nagy was a total artist of the stage, concerned with the achievements of novel effects through perspective, color and lighting. After coming from Hungary he taught at the Julius Hartt Foundation in Connecticut. In 1939 he organized the Theater Model Museum at Yale University, and later received Rockefeller grants for work in theater.

In this time of change it was concluded that a single opera production would be wise, and with Mae West due in August for *Diamond Lil*, there was a certainty of a financially strong season.

Though he knew little of the Central City Opera House history, had seen none of the Jones or Graf-Oenslager-Cooper-St. Leger productions, Nagy had his own definite ideas. *Die Fledermaus* had not yet been presented at The Met, and was then something of a rarity. Although some of the casting was off, it was a generally fresh version which stayed clear of the vulgarization of subsequent productions.

With her roguishly acted and liltingly sung Adele, Adelaide Bishop was enchanting. As Rosalinda, Regina Resnick displayed a grace and vocal elegance which *Fidelio* had not drawn on. Suave Clifford Harvuot headed a group of personable men including the astute Norman Kelley, handsome Davis Cunningham, and commanding Kenneth Schoen.

Nagy directed and did both sets and costumes. Peter Herman Adler came as musical director. A few years later Adler would bring renown to NBC with his televised opera productions. Just where St. Leger stood in production "arrangements" was never clarified. He was never seen at Central City that summer.

The theatrical offering was the suave Molnar comedy, *The Play's The Thing*, done in P.G. Wodehouse's witty adaptation, acted in impeccable style by Louis Calhern and Faye Emerson, under the direction of Broadway's Gilbert Miller.

For the 1950 season, Nagy scheduled two firsts. Puccini's *Madama Butterfly* and Donizetti's *Don Pasquale* were strong extensions of repertory, operas that would be repeated numerous times, so well did they fit into the scheme of Central City opera.

Another Hungarian, a young conductor, Tibor Kozma, joined Nagy, who as before did the sets and costumes and the direction. St. Leger was absent, though again, as in 1949, given credit for "arrangements."

A brilliantly conceived *Don Pasquale* was a merry surprise. Its prologue offered chess figures singing the chorus normally sung in the third act by the servants. Fine-edged performances by Adelaide Bishop as Norina, Clifford Harvuot, a polished Malatesta; Davis Cunningham an ideally personable Ernesto, and Stanley Carlson a blustery Don gave the audience characters to relish, along with Nagy's charming settings.

Virgil Thomson found the musical textures under Tibor Kozma's direction "steely, hard, and more than a little coarse." This was a matter St. Leger would surely have caught.

For the first Puccini opera to be done at Central City, Nagy provided freshly conceived stage action and splendid settings which involved audiences in the melodrama.

The popular play was Shaw's *The Devil's Disciple* starring the great Shakespearean, Maurice Evans, with John Williams a superb General Burgoyne, and Helen Bonfils in a tiny role.

1951 was designated a Diamond Jubilee, marking 20 years since the 1952 opening but 16 years of actual Festivals.

For this occasion, the Association stretched itself to do four operatic productions, including a revival of the 1950 hit *Don Pasquale*, a double bill of Menotti's *Amelia Goes To The Ball* with Eleanor Steber and *The Beautiful Galatea*, the Von Suppe operetta, and Gounod's *Romeo and Juliet*.

This meant a heavy schedule for conductor Tibor Kozma, so orchestral niceties were missed while Kozma drove his brass for inappropriate drama. He lacked a lyric impulse. Nagy could not handle all responsibilities, even though he had Irene Kahn, who was almost never seen without a delighted smile, as his invaluable assistant. Director Alfred de Liagre, Jr., who had enjoyed a Broadway success with *The Voice of the Turtle*, came to do the double bill in his first operatic experience, and it showed. Oenslager designed the double bill.

The idea of joining the Menotti with the Von Suppe didn't work. Both were frivolous but in different keys of farce, and de Liagre's tentative direction of each compounded this problem. The Menotti lacked theatrical definition, and Steber seemed strident, both vocally and dramatically. Oenslager's handsome draw curtain and a rich period setting provided a beguiling Central City ambience, but that was about it. Kozma's musical direction was unsubtle. The Viennese *Galatea* had been staged for cuteness and broad humor where it needed glamour and wit.

Adelaide Bishop was straining to do both Norina in the revived *Pasquale* and learning the heavy Juliet role. Things piled up on her, and she ended up singing a Juliet at Friday's dress rehearsal and at the Saturday opening, and again on Sunday afternoon when her alternate, Virginia Haskins, was ill. Haskins's delayed debut on Tuesday evening was worth waiting for, as she was a delicate yet exacting performer of great beauty.

The matter of dress rehearsals was a long tradition at Central City. It brought an opportunity to express to statewide media and other supporters of the Association an appreciation of that important sustenance. Singers would be those scheduled for the Sunday matinee which meant the surprise of hearing a lesser known talent who on occasion would surpass a better known name.

Gounod's *Romeo and Juliet* was for the most part strongly cast with such male stalwarts as Clifford Harvuot and Andrew Gainey as alternate Mercutios, Francesco Valentino as Capulet, and Davis Cunningham both handsome and mellow as one Romeo. The other was David Garen, a too inexperienced tenor. There were also the wandering pitches of the Bulgarian bass, Lubomir Vichegonov, later known as Lubomir Vichey. Margaret Roggero was a strong nurse.

At the invitation of the Association, a large assemblage of national music critics attended the opening. I was assigned by *The Denver Post* where I was then writing to do a series of brief interviews regarding the Romeo during the intermission.

"In this opera house," Alfred Frankenstein of *The San Francisco Chronicle* told me, "the production has the advantage of intimacy. I'm fascinated with its being given in English. There is no straining to understand, and the opera has been beautifully and imaginatively staged."

Virgil Thomson, out for *The New York Herald-Tribune*, observed that "It's a very tricky opera to perform, and it steadily increased in effectiveness during this first-night performance." He also told me "there is no passion - the opera has no balls."

For Albert Goldberg of *The Los Angeles Times* it was a "fine staging of an old opera. Both soprano Adelaide Bishop and the tenor, Davis Cunningham, were excellent. They have nice, fresh voices, and the scenery is original instead of the stuffy, old-fashioned kind we're used to."

Prior to the opening, Olin Downes had used a Sunday column of *The New York Times* to object to something he had read by Nagy about curbing the sweetness of the Gounod with angular, sombre settings in order to avoid "the unbearable sweetness, like a cup of coffee with five lumps of sugar." Despite these words, his sets were highly romantic and not untraditional, so this was a pointless annoyance of Downes. Nagy's words did not agree with his design execution.

The hit of the season was again *Don Pasquale*, more engaging than ever because of Carlton Gauld's roguish yet subtle playing of the lead. The production was again outstanding.

This season the play was expected to be pre-eminent, with Katharine Cornell's imposing appearance in Maugham's *The Constant Wife* along with dapper Brian Aherne and elegant Grace George. The supposed humor of the play never became spontaneous, and its arch humor made the production seem aloof. Its high-style had been worked over by director Guthrie McClintock and in combination with the overburdened setting by Oenslager was somewhat charmless.

Charles Laughton attended a performance to receive cheers from the audience as he was recognized just after intermission. He was there to see Gertrude Musgrove of the cast who was the wife of Vincent Korda, a former associate.

When *Time* commented on the 1951 season it reported a budget of $110,000 for four productions and a deficit of $265. *Time* went on to quote Nagy, "The only trouble with Central City is that there aren't a hundred of them."

Well before the opening of the 1952 season, Nagy was quoted as saying that "*Macbeth* is the opera I would most like to do next season." Lee Casey's reaction was never recorded, nor did he express alarm that *La Boheme* would be done in 1952. *Macbeth* would not be done until 1988.

At the announcement that Mae West would bring *Diamond Lil* to Central City, Casey had written in the *Rocky Mountain News* "Mae's just right for Central City. Let us hope that the choice means that those in charge of affairs at Central City have recovered from the artiness that deterred so many from attending performances in the old mining camp. I'd like to see a revival of *Floradora* or *The Prince of Pilsen* or *Babes in Toyland*."

There was art there in 1952 - Mozart and Puccini- despite Casey's digs.

With illustrious hopes, *The Marriage of Figaro*, to be designed and directed by Nagy, and *La Boheme*, to be designed by Oenslager and staged by Frank St. Leger, his first directorial work for Central City since the 1936 *Gondoliers*, would make a luminous season.

It had been decided to have the two teams since each production demanded such special attention. The public was interested in the season's billings, and by three weeks prior to the opening it was reported that 40% of the seats had been sold.

Memorable bounties filled Nagy's *Figaro* production. Anne Bollinger's affecting Countess, Frances Bible's mercurial Cherubino, James Pease's splendid Figaro, and Virginia MacWatters' sprightly Susanna all set the opera well. Kosma's conducting was jet-propelled and graceless. The success of the production came from the strength of its casting and its fine baroque settings.

Alex Murphree described the production well: "Dr. Nagy has a genius for the baroque, for brightness, gusto, elegance, and charm. Everything about the production seemed to laugh, the high spirits of the music and of the characters being amplified by the high key of the colors, all yellows, pearl whites, pinks, and golds reinforcing golds."

The handsome scenes which Nagy devised for *Figaro* were interrupted by a frequent lowering of the curtain, a scene-changing miscalculation which was more cumbersome than it ought to have been. Backstage facilities were still primitive, with no proper scenery loft. With four acts and as many sets and an effort to avoid having three intermissions the decision to have but one intermission was made. It seemed that Kozma rushed tempos in order to bring the final curtain down as early as he could.

The restraint of St. Leger's production made *La Boheme* very moving. Oenslager outdid himself in the grays, blue-grays, and gray-greens of his settings, with the wintry branches of a great tree bringing memorable beauty to Act III.

The Mimis were four, with the lovely Anne Bollinger, the sensitive Ann Ayers, and the pert Virginia MacWatters and the unimpressive Brenda Miller. James MacCracken made a notable debut as Rodolfo, showing the voice of great natural beauty that won him popularity for so many years. On a Tuesday well into the run David Poleri made his debut as a super-charged tenor who was having some problems singing in English an opera he had learned in Italian. It took him three tries to blow out the candle in Act I.

He was a Rodolfo who unwrapped the fish brought by Schaunard for the Bohemians's celebration to hold up the newspaper wrapping to exclaim, "Ah, *The Denver Post*." Hugh Thompson was a solid Marcello, and there were a few Collines by James Pease, though Michael Bondon did most of these. Kozma's Puccini fared better than his Mozart.

Following these significant productions with the wonderful Helen Hayes in the small-scaled *Mrs. McThing* by Denver's Mary Chase may have seemed anti-climactic. This whimsical fluff was not for all tastes, but Miss Hayes attracted a strong attendance. Among those in the cast was Frank Corsaro who subsequently moved into opera direction, and returned in 1970 to direct *La Boheme* and *Of Mice and Men*.

There were those, Lee Casey not among them, who believed an opera house had an obligation to do *Carmen*. In any case, 1953 would be the year. Herbert Graf returned to direct, with Oenslager doing the sets, but there was no Frank St. Leger to balance things out.

Nagy would concentrate on designing and directing *The Merry Wives of Windsor*. Kurt Adler, chorus director at The Met would conduct both operas.

The program described *Carmen* as "A new American version by Paul Green," best known for such pageantry as *The Lost Colony* prepared for production at Jamestown, Virginia. His major innovation was in a new scene at the beginning of Act IV, loosely adapted from a scene in the Prosper Merrimee novel,where Don Jose enters a church to pray for "the soul of one unworthy to die."

*Carmen*, the most difficult of all operas to get right, seemed to be the wrong opera for Graf, for he failed to ignite the work with those sensuous touches which *Carmen* so desperately requires. The elements did not mesh. It was in turn realistic, sultry, sombre. It was compelling only in its third act, this largely because of Florence Lamont Hinman's fine chorus.

The final act was gussied up with elements of commedia dell'arte, picadors on hobby horses, and a laughable lack of proportion. There was also a disparity in Oenslager's designs. The set for Acts I and IV were crowded and seemed to have been designed for a much larger stage than that at Central City, a very unusual slip for Oenslager.

Graf seemed not to recognize the powerful psychological structure of the opera, and conductor Adler was another who went for superficiality.

Olin Downes, Music Editor and critic of *The New York Times*, wrote two lengthy Sunday articles in which he expressed critical indignation, writing of a "vandalistic handling of its finale." Though he objected strenuously to Green's tampering with the final act, he supported the restoration of spoken dialogue. He found the translation flavorless, but it was the concept that he disliked.

"The Graf version is bad enough," he wrote, "to be the subject of protest, and to point a moral to the tale of opera producers whose one purpose seems to be a desire at any cost, to appear as innovators, with bad new ideas to substitute for good old ones."

Mildred Miller he thought a superficial, unconvincing Carmen, but he did admire Lucine Amara as Micaela in one of her early professional appearances. He thought Adler conducted with "authority and dramatic sense."

Fortunately there was Nagy's engagingly fresh *Merry Wives of Windsor* to balance out the *Carmen*. Nagy saw to it that its style carried through in deftly turned costumes and settings. The production was airy, filled with appealing detail and engaging characterizations.

As happens so frequently, illness beset the cast, and on the opening night ailing Virginia MacWatters was replaced by Jacqueline Moody as Mistress Ford to be hailed by Alex Murphree in the *Post*. By the time Olin Downes attended this production he could write that "The most brilliant member of the cast is Virginia MacWatters who companions the brilliancy and effectiveness of her song with the art of an accomplished comedienne."

Downes described the production as one to be "ranked as one of the most distinguished and delightful productions that the Central City Opera Festival has given in many seasons."

"So appropriate is this production," he continued, "with its flavor of the Elizabethan theater in decor and stage business, and the contagious spirit of the interpretation that instead of ranking as a respectful historical revival of opera of the past, this presentation of the *Merry Wives* takes on the character of a 'find' on the part of the constantly enterprising and creative-spirited Central City."

Despite his harsh views on *Carmen*, Downes maintained a genuine affection for Central City, particularly when it was at its best as in the *Wives*, and later attempted to describe the unique character of the enterprise:

"For them (the audience)," he wrote, "the opera has what it should have for all of us, a very human and romantic appeal. And there, where we once saw cowboys drive their horses into the bar, and order drinks while mounted; there where, perhaps a little self-consciously but with real loyalty to their town, they keep the old opera house, the old buildings, shacks, railroad sidings and mine tailings much as they were in the old days - there they heartily love music, take it to themselves with huge relish, and patronize their opera to the limit, so far as we could see, of the seating capacity of the house. It is a heartening experience to sit with them."

The play which followed was Arthur Laurents' *The Time of the Cuckoo* with Shirley Booth, whose skilled comic sense made it a true hit. In the spring she had won a Tony award for her performance in the play, and her face had adorned *Time* during its successful New York run. Not long before that she had taken an Oscar for *Come Back, Little Sheba*, so there was real celebrity on stage. Towards the end, Mary Astor came to Central City to rehearse for the national tour that would follow when Shirley Booth returned to Hollywood.

There was increasing support on the Board for the idea of doing one old and one new or little-known opera. The kind of contrast that was considered appropriate was planned for 1954 with *Faust* and *Ariadne auf Naxos*, the Richard Strauss amalgam of commedia dell'arte and romantic opera.

This was not the first proposal. At the conclusion of the 1953 season there had been talk of doing such musical theater as *Kiss Me Kate*, *Carousel*, or *The Beggar's Opera*. Rick's Board would need another reminder of his goals.

When *Ariadne* was announced, L.M. Pexton. prominent Denver businessman and Central City supporter, wrote to the *Post* of his concern that the opera was obscure. But in the *Post's* Alex Murphree the opera found a champion who would write, "I find it musically the most exciting opera I have heard in nine season."

There were strong vocal elements in Virginia MacWatters' delectable Zerbinetta, and the utterly delightful singing of her fantastic aria, with Eva Likova a lovely Ariadne, as well as on some evenings a fine Composer, while Polyna Stoska gave splendor to the Composer in later performances.

A new team was on board for *Ariadne*, with Dino Yannapoulos, Met stage director, and Lemuel Ayers, a distinguished Broadway designer. Kurt Adler conducted in his second season. Yannapoulos was overheard telling people at a post-opening party that he didn't know what the opera was all about, so it seemed he was the wrong one to make the effort. Its complications lacked satirical edge but there was some lovely singing and acting.

Ayers designed handsomely for the prologue but the opera set diminished the size of the stage.

*Faust* was Nagy's show, a superb designer's work, triumphant in its intricate neo-Baroque style and studied proportions. Adler's laggard tempos slowed things down but there were potent Fausts in Jon Crain and Brian Sullivan, and a moving Marguerite by Virginia MacWatters though a lesser one by a miscast Adelaide Bishop.

Theodore Uppman as Valentin gave the first of several fine performances which made him a Central City favorite. Frances Bible returned to shine as Siebel. A *Faust* without a Mephistopheles can't make it. Lubomir Vichegonov not only failed to seem awesome or diabolical, he was vocally wobbly and dramatically pop-eyed.

The 1954 play was *The Caine Mutiny Court Martial*, exciting in its melodramatic appeal and the strength of its all-male cast. Paul Douglas, from sportscasting and films, was Captain Queeg, and Wendell Corey, also of films, was Greenwald, all solidly directed by Charles Laughton, and enthusiastically received.

Corey had the misfortune to trip on the boardwalk near the Teller House following the opening night performance, and sprained his ankle, so he performed mostly in a cast.

For some years the Association had been dickering with the D'Oyly Carte Opera Company for a season of Gilbert and Sullivan at Central City, and in 1955 that finally came about, with four weeks of *The Mikado, Yeoman of the Guard, Iolanthe*, and a double bill of *Trial By Jury* and *H.M.S. Pinafore*.

Although this would be a departure from the creative aspects of Central City opera, audiences relished these productions from a company in fine shape which gave splendid style to these popular works. *Yeoman* had been a hit in 1939. These productions showed musical theater on a superb, wholly professional basis which represented the kind of singing and playing to which the Association always aspired.

Such singers as Peter Pratt, Donald Adams, Fisher Morgan, Ann Drummond-Grant, with Isadore Godfrey to conduct, gave scintillating displays of their classic renditions of the great G & S roles. *Iolanthe* was the supreme triumph. And the opera house was again proven ideal for such musical theater.

The play was William Inge's *Bus Stop* in which Albert Salmi downed a quart of milk nightly, in one gulp, and Peggy Ann Garner was a poignant co-star.

Aspirations were high at Central City following the superb season of Gilbert and Sullivan, which all had to admit was an importation. But things were going on which would place the Central City Opera on the national scene with a new and higher significance.

# THE BALLAD OF BABY DOE

As the years passed, Ricketson was taking a stronger lead in urging production of an original opera on a regional subject. Ricketson responded favorably to an inquiry by composer Douglas Moore about interest in a new opera on Colorado materials. Earlier Moore had approached the Koussevitzky Foundation at the Library of Congress, a modestly endowed source of support for many composers. It could offer Moore no more than $2,000, which would provide Columbia University, where Moore was a professor of composition, with a work of celebration for its 1954 centennial.

Moore did not believe he could proceed on the arduous work of creating an opera on so little, so looked to Central City for additional support.

Moore had been fascinated by a faded 1933 newspaper clipping which detailed the discovery of the frozen body of Baby Doe Tabor in a cabin at the Matchless Mine near Leadville. The more that Moore studied the clipping, the more certain he was there was an opera in it.

Elizabeth McCourt Doe while married to Harvey Doe and living in Central City was popularly known as Baby Doe. In Leadville she met the vigorous mining and construction leader H.A.W.Tabor. Before coming West from his native Vermont he married Augusta Pierce in her native Maine, and the two had joined the Westward movement. They had become just about the most respected and wealthy citizens of Leadville.

The meeting of Tabor and Baby Doe seemed an act of destiny. After obtaining a secret divorce in Durango he subsequently married Baby Doe in a private ceremony in St. Louis, after which he settled Baby Doe in an apartment in his Windsor Hotel in Denver. Here he endeavored to achieve social acceptance for her but was unable to break through into the upper crust.

While Tabor was serving a 30-day term as Senator, he and Baby Doe were again married in Washington, D.C. with President Arthur in attendance. Tabor's luck fell with the changing of national monetary policy. The ultimate collapse of the Colorado mining industry brought him financial ruin. He never would sell his first major mine, The Matchless at Leadville, and always urged Baby Doe to hold on to it. After his death in 1899, Baby Doe moved to the mine shanty where she was found dead on March 7, 1935.

It was no wonder script writers and novelists were attracted to the story of these people. In 1932, Warner Brothers released the film *Silver Dollar* which cast Edward G. Robinson in a Tabor-like role, with Bebe Daniels in the Baby Doe role, and Aline McMahon as the first wife. No actual names were used.

With encouragement from Ricketson, Douglas Moore got in touch with Paul Green, 1927 Pulitzer Prize winner for his play *In Abraham's Bosom*. Later he wrote the pageant *The Lost Colony* as well as several other historical pageants. For Central City in 1953 he had done the controversial English adaptation of *Carmen*, along with the questionable interpolation of Act IV, Scene 1.

By March 1954 Green claimed to have done three- quarters of the book. In April when Moore read through the supposedly complete libretto he found it unusable for his purposes. Herbert Graf, who had been asked to take a look at it, since he had wished to direct the production at Central City, also thought it did not work. Ultimately Graf did not figure in the production that would be done, because it was felt his outlook was too European.

Green remained anxious to do the opera, and let it be known he was dissatisfied with Moore's earlier operas, and thought he could do better finding his own composer.

In Denver, Caroline Bancroft, regional writer of pamphlets on Colorado historical topics, learned of Green's project on Baby Doe. Since it was she who had uncovered a great many hitherto unknown facts about Baby Doe, which she had used in an imagined first- person narrative, hers was a strongly proprietary interest.

Miss Bancroft had indeed written some scenes of a play on the subject , adapted from her writings. She now expressed a desire to collaborate with Green on an opera libretto, making certain that history, and her work in uncovering it, would stay intact.

In letters to the Association following the breach between himself and Moore, Green implied that he was a dramatist and not an historian. He feared his dramatic structure would suffer in deference to facts. Green had drawn on some material he could have obtained only from Miss Bancroft's booklets, for there were as well her publications on Augusta and H.A.W. Tabor.

The Association chose to dissolve its relationship with Green. Miss Bancroft then offered to come on board as Historical Adviser on the Tabor opera and received an honorarium of $250.

In the face of a possible suit by Miss Bancroft, Green withdrew from any involvement in the opera. At this point matters involving "The Tabor Opera," as it was then known, looked bleak.

A sudden development led to John Latouche, who turned out to be the catalyst capable of resolving the problems. Because of the theatrical acumen he had shown in several successes, he was signed in September 1954 to write the libretto.

Latouche had enjoyed two Broadway triumphs successes, both musicals. The first in 1940, *Cabin In The Sky* with music by Vernon Duke and lyrics by Ted Fetter, gave Ethel Waters, Katherine Dunham and Dooley Wilson a major hit, In 1955 *The Golden Apples* was well received. He had also been one of the many, along with poets Dorothy Parker and Richard Wilbur, who worked on the lyrics for *Candide*, the Leonard Bernstein-Lillian Hellman musical which opened in December 1956.

Ricketson personally advanced Moore and Latouche $40,000 for the project, one in which he believed deeply, which in turn convinced the Board of the project's potential. In November 1954 at the Association annual meeting it was announced that "The Tabor Opera" would open at Central City in the 1956 Festival season.

Moore and Latouche complemented each other. Moore was the calm patrician, a warm, charming man while Latouche had his own earthy charm, somewhat on the roguish side. Moore was tall and ruddy while Latouche was short and pudgy with eyes which seemed to take everything in.

Latouche brought to the collaboration a feeling for dramatic pulse which Moore admired, and this overrode what other problems arose. More importantly, Latouche provided exactly the sentimental center which the two-handkerchief opera needed, one which would make of Augusta a figure of sympathy, turn Baby Doe into an object of ultimate admiration, and preserve for Tabor some dignity.

The collaborators came from different worlds, and neither would have sought out the other as a friend, but here they were, building a world together, an opera which in its fourth decade continues to work its appeal on audiences.

When Latouche came to Denver for the final preparations preceding the opening he made a point of calling on Caroline Bancroft to let her know how helpful her writings had been to him in setting a tone for the book, as well in filling out the characters of Baby Doe and Augusta. She kindly responded with suggestions for further humanizing the roles of the principals.

Latouche deferred to her judgement in removing from the first scene the Chinese porter who tags along with Baby Doe's luggage as she arrives at Leadville, a correction of history since there were no Chinese servants in the Colorado mining camps. He also altered a reference from "49-ers" to "59-ers."

At a Board meeting in October 1955, music from the opera was played and sung for the first time, and on October 14 the Board made a unanimous decision to present what by now had come to be known as *The Ballad of Baby Doe* at the 1956 Festival.

Donald Oenslager was asked to design the production, an elaborate one, calling for 11 scenes over its two acts. This demanding presentation would benefit from the new $50,000 fly loft for backdrops and other scenic pieces. Oenslager was an obvious choice because of his feeling for Colorado, derived from many years of work at Central City and visits in Colorado Springs, a favored locale.

Emerson Buckley, conductor of the New York City Opera, and a former student at Columbia University of Douglas Moore, was chosen as one who would bring to the performances the care and energy it required.

The great Broadway hit of the previous season was *My Fair Lady*, and its unstilted choreography by Hanya Holm was thought to be a major element in its success. Through many summers spent teaching dance at Colorado College in Colorado Springs she had become somewhat knowledgeable about Colorado. Although she had never directed an opera she was signed on as a co-director. In the staging of musical numbers and dances for such other stage works as *My Darlin' Aida* and *Kiss Me Kate*, she had won acclaim, but these were totally different from the demands of opera and its disciplines.

The program would read "The production staged by Hanya Holm. Edwin Levy, Co-Director." Levy was the single Colorado participant in the production. He had extensive operatic directing experience in staging *Madama Butterfly*, *Salome*, and *Rigoletto* for the Greater Denver Opera Association at the Tabor Grand Opera House, an apt connection. In addition he staged many operas for the University of Denver Theater, as well as five operettas and musical comedies staged in Cheesman Park under the auspices of The Denver Post. These included *The Red Mill*, *South Pacific*, *Oklahoma*, *Carousel*, and *The Music Man*.

Hanya Holm's concern, she told me in an interview, was with "keying movement to the expressive elements of the music rather than having indiscriminate use of operatic gestures and stances." Levy was in perfect agreement. The difference was that Hanya Holm did not read operatic scores but Levy did.

Buckley was understandably nervous over the musical aspects, as he was determined to have an exciting performance to impress the many visitors expected for the opening. He often lost his temper in rehearsal. He knew of the large potential of the work, and he never lost the opportunity to speak well of it.

Oenslager was a calming influence, for that was his temper. His work, and there had been much of it in so large a production, was almost entirely done. There were costuming problems in the Windsor Hotel scene, for both Dolores Wilson and Leyna Gabriele, the Baby Does, disliked their mutton-sleeved ball gowns, whose wide ribbons fell in cumbersome fashion from the shoulder. Each devised a different way of handling these heavy, wide hangings.

There was also a musical problem in this scene, for the aria "Wake Snakes" which Baby Doe sings to Mama McCourt made no sense to the singers, and worse, gave them the giggles. Happily, this was replaced with the stirring aria in which Baby Doe refers to "the fine ladies" who "walk with their heads held high," far more to the point, and dramatically suitable.

The opening night was one of high-styled brilliance. Critics from across the nation were there. Lucius Beebe parked his private railroad car in Denver and ascended to Central City. New York theatrical producer Michael Myerberg who was seriously contemplating a New York production of the opera joined the throng.

Though there were some who dreaded what they might hear, it was a triumph. There were others of course who believed Colorado had more elevating history to sing about, and a minority complained of a lack of melody.

I have my own memories of that opening night. Augusta's tender streak was affectingly shown as she emerges from the Tabor Opera House to sing "I like Adelina Patti, she sings divinely," a phrase of melting beauty as sung by Frances Bible, the supreme Augusta of them all.

The tintype of Augusta and her gossiping friends, Tabor lost in a tumble of memories backstage at the Tabor Opera House in Denver, and most eloquently Baby Doe establishing in her final aria that, disruptive as her life had been, in the end it was more than worth the pain.

Walter Cassel was Tabor come to life. There never has been a better, truer Tabor, so robust and romantic, and in the final scene, such a dreamer, if by then little else.

Dolores Wilson sang the arias beautifully, but lacked the ability to quicken hearts through her acting ability. It appeared that tenderness was missing in her persona, and she walked through some scenes like an automaton.

In the assay office adjacent to the Teller House I was typing my opening night review late in the evening when Walter Cassel knocked at the window to wave at me, not wanting any more than the rest of us to let such exhilaration slip away.

During the performance, Campton Bell, the erudite chairman of the University of Denver Theater Department, was overheard as a nervous stagehand retrieved a very visibly misplaced pillar from the Tabor backstage scene, one left over from Augusta's palatial Pasadena parlor, "Stop, they're stealing the scenery."

At the conclusion the stage was heavy with the tiny traditional bouquets tossed from the audience to the cast on stage. Cast and directors and designers gathered to receive applause, and cameras shot the scene. *The Ballad of Baby Doe* had been assembled and delivered in a fine hour of creativity by the Central City Opera.

One month to a day after the premiere John Latouche was found dead at his desk of a heart attack, stricken as he worked to complete revisions. He had completed "The fine ladies," an important new scene for Tabor and his cronies in which he urges support for William Jennings Bryan's gold policy, or "Turn tail and run." Tabor's ardor was firmly established with the new and beautiful "Warm as an autumn night" aria for the second scene. As though working on borrowed time, Latouche rounded up the loose ends, and that was all.

Douglas Moore went on to admired operas, *Carry Nation* and, from Henry James, *The Wings of a Dove*, both well received by critics, but already neglected. Moore died July 26, 1969.

The scenery for the 11 scenes cost $15,522, and costumes were $15,453, with a total production cost of $112,674.

Such critics as Roger Dettmer of the *Chicago Sun* were bothered by Moore and Latouche's rejection of the currently fashionable musical devices of Berg and Schoenberg; Dettmer affirmed they had "produced a mouse." Howard Taubman in *The New York Times* was wholeheartedly enthusiastic.

Following the New York City Opera production in 1958, Winthrop Sergeant of *The New Yorker* became a major supporter. He wrote of "the beauty of Mr. Moore's music, together with Latouche's skill at drawing character (which) relieves it of any suggestion of banality." He also praised Moore for what he termed "a declaration of independence - independence from all the fashionable highbrow fiddle-faddle and mysterious mumbo-jumbo that during the past forty years have tended to reduce the art of opera to a feeble caricature of itself."

When *Baby Doe* was premiered in New York Beverly Sills took what became one of her best roles, with Walter Cassel repeating his dynamic Tabor. Martha Lipton did Augusta which she had done at Central City but without the bite and character detail provided by Frances Bible, who later would take on the role for New York City Opera. It is a blessing that the recording brings us Sills, Bible, and Cassel in their classic performances.

Vladimir Rosing's staging was generally thought to be flat, but the opera was enthusiastically received, and since then has been in and out of the repertory. The original Central City scenery was used in the first several years of performances in New York.

# TOSCA AND OTHERS

Because Sardou had so entitled his drama, it was *La Tosca* which alternated with *Baby Doe*. Elemer Nagy outdid himself in stagecraft. There was vivid drama in the climax of Act I with Scarpia singing out in the church of his lust for Tosca, while movement, color and light built up a wild crescendo.

Back in 1954 Mrs. Penrose had been so impressed by the sheen of Lucine Amara's soprano that she personally aided her studies. Now that Amara was Tosca at Central City she was definitely at center stage. Despite tameness in her dramatic projection, the consistent velvet in her voice gave distinction to a lavish production.

Highly detailed characterization was always a mark of Frank Guarrera's performances, of which there would be nine between 1956 and 1974 in Central City. As Scarpia he labored over his makeup, which oddly enough resulted in his being a deadringer for conductor Saul Caston of the Denver Symphony Orchestra. Mostly he sang well, although forcing brought forth a wobble.

There was an Angelotti worth attending to in the splendid Norman Treigle who already possessed the intensity which would mark his tragically short career. Cornell MacNeil made a strong Central City debut as an alternate Scarpia, while as other Toscas there was the vivacious Mariquita Moll and the Denver soprano, Willabelle Underwood, a protege of Florence Lamont Hinman.

Jon Crain came down with a cold, so newcomer John Druary exhibited his nice, nimble tenor, without the heroic metal of Crain's big voice. Emerson Buckley conducted with authority and sweep. Nagy's ornate production cost $70,158.73.

Howard Taubman wrote in *The New York Times* that " the quality of the singing makes the deepest impression," and elsewhere he found the young American singers providing a "vocal glamour that would have astonished the early settlers in these parts."

Ideal theatrical pleasures were granted by *The Lark*, Lillian Hellman's adaptation of the Jean Anouilh drama with the luminous Julie Harris notable as Joan of Arc. Joseph Anthony masterfully directed a strong case including George Macready, Sam Jaffe, who had been in the 1937 Central City *A Doll's House*, Leo Ciceri, and Tammy Grimes in a small part. It was in Central City during the run of *The Lark* that actor Christopher Plummer, who played the Dauphin in the Broadway production, married Miss Grimes.

The perennial wish to do something new in the house led up strange alleys. At the annual meeting in 1956 there was talk of commissioning an opera to be based on John Ford's classic western *Stagecoach*, to be known as *Stagecoach to Central City*, but nothing came of it.

Again there were the yearly suggestions of *Brigadoon* or *Kiss Me Kate*, but Ricketson told the Board, "musical comedy is not our field - - -if selling tickets were our only consideration we should probably replace the chorus with the Oklahoma football team."

Doing the unique was sometimes a strain on the chosen course. Dr. Nagy hailed from Montenegro in Hungary, so he thought that the Strauss *Gypsy Baron* would charm with its beguiling score. Its bulky libretto refused ministrations. It was a dud that refused to come to life. If ever the music could be freed from the dull constraints of its book, the world would become a more charming place.

Maria di Gerlando was a beauty with a lustrous soprano, and Yul Brynner's vivacious sister, Vera, was a charming alternate in one of her very few stage performances.

*Rigoletto* would probably have made Lee Casey's list of forbidden works, but there it was, elegantly designed by Nagy, with a high balcony for a stage band in Act I which served as a kind of Bridge of Sighs for Count Monterone to cross to his imprisonment in Act III.

Frank Guarrera, Cornell MacNeil, and Hugh Thompson alternated in the heavy lead role. I heard a tired Guarrera in a performance most interesting for the beguiling if slightly mature Gilda of Virginia MacWatters. Again Jon Crain and John Druary alternated as Dukes of Mantua, but neither was a convincing rake.

The 1957 season was the last for Nagy, his ninth. In these nine years he had invigorated the repertory with such true delights as *Don Pasquale* and *The Merry Wives of Windsor*, and had brought brilliant productions of *The Marriage of Figaro* and *Tosca*. He was proud of diversifying the repertory with his meticulously mounted productions.

There was a sense that the field of education was the challenge to which his ideas led him, as compared with the transient pleasures of public, professional performance.

The 1957 season had been beset with enough problems to drive anyone from the field. Hugh Thompson, a baritone, one night became a tenor because both Davis Cunningham and John Druary were voiceless with laryngitis. Osie Hawkins stepped in on opening night for Ralph Herbert for a role he learned on the spur of the moment. Virginia MacWatters again missed an opening night when voiceless at the *Rigoletto* opening, Irene Jordan stepped in for her. The University of Colorado was said to be reviewing the cause of these viral infections.

Nagy had been experimenting with scenic devices, and developed a revolutionary system of projecting designs onto plexiglass panels, and worked to expand its usage. He used it himself when he took over the Opera Workshop at the Aspen Music School in the early 60s for a production of *The Magic Flute*. His death at 65 in August 1971 was sudden and a great loss to opera.

For 1958 the Association scheduled that great hit of the Metropolitan season, *La Perichole*, and for the first time, that popular combination, opera's "ham and eggs," *I Pagliacci* and *Cavalleria Rusticana*.

# MERRILL'S DEBUT

Gold was struck with Offenbach's choice *La Perichole*. Cyril Ritchard came to star in it and to stage it, with Nathaniel Merrill at Central City for the first time as nominal stage director. Rolf Gerard's smart sets were cut down to size from those he had done at The Met. Six principals from that production saw to it that the style was ready-made and glittering, which made it less than a Central City production in the true sense.

Most importantly it was found that *La Perichole* belonged in the Central City Opera House as nowhere else. Perfection like this had not been seen before.

Ritchard did his high-class music hall act. Lois Hunt was a quite irresistible Perichole and Theodore Uppman came into his own as a golden-voiced Paquillo. Such character singers as Osie Hawkins and Paul Franke and actor Arthur Malet as the Prisoner were engaging presences in a gay romp. Fun such as this could not go wrong.

In *The Lively Arts* I wrote that "it was paced like a winged steed, spicy as an East Indian market, it has the elegance of a Parisian boulevardier. Thoroughly professional in every aspect, *Perichole* has been lavished with more scrupulous preparation than any production in Central City annals, and it shows. The perceptible touch of perfection makes it shine like a Mediterranean travel poster."

Whatever was alternating with *Perichole's* giddy good nature would have been at a disadvantage, but a heavily conventional production of operatic standbys was surely self-defeating.

There was supposed to has been vocal glamour from Herva Nelli, Toscanini's Aida and Desdemona and Alice from his famed broadcasts who had signed on as Santuzza, but she canceled. Gloria Lind was a pallid substitute. There was John Alexander in an auspicious debut, still another fine talent on his way to The Met. Helen Vanni dazzled as Lois, but this Hans Busch production never came to life.

*I Pagliacci* fared somewhat better with a fervent Jon Crain as Canio and Clifford Harvuot a compelling Tonio, but again this production built up little steam. Some orchestral excitement came from Buckley and the musicians but Busch, from Indiana University and a member of the great musical family, seemed to have overly academic credentials. Rolf Gerard's sets were being tried out for a new Met production but at Central City they were merely drab.

At $158,069.63, costs for 1958 were high. Surprisingly, in view of the popularity and admiration for the Offenbach operetta, ticket sales were down from the previous year to $130,214.30. The margin between expenses and profit was starting to widen.

The play was *And Perhaps Happiness*, Thomas Hornsby Ferril's verse drama, winner of a competition sponsored by *The Denver Post* for which Ferril won $10,000.

Edwin Levy, the only director other than Robert Edmond Jones to stage both opera and theater at Central City, directed a cast which included the fine Barbara O'Neil, Mrs. O'Hara from *Gone With The Wind*, Hugh Marlowe and K.T. Stevens from films, Richard Gaines, and Barbara Moore, a descendent of Territorial Governor John Evans and of Anne Evans, lovely in a small role, were others who brightened the stage.

Oenslager again provided Colorado backgrounds with his distinctive sense of design, but the wordy, inconclusive play, with often puzzling motivation, overpowered the virtues in the production. It was a worthy effort which misfired because of the author's unfamiliarity with stage techniques.

Again it was time to try out a new production team. There was no interest in going back to Hans Busch. This time it was Nathaniel Merrill who had so brightly expanded on Ritchard's ideas in *Perichole*, and was largely responsible for its sleekness and pizzazz who would be named stage director, with Robert O'Hearn as stage designer for the 1959 season.

Together they would move productions towards greater sophistication in movement and design. O'Hearn had been chief assistant to Oliver Smith on the designing of *My Fair Lady* and thus was expert in stage craft. He knew how to provide strong dramatic atmospheres, and was proficient with revolving stages. Together, he and Merrill had worked at the New England Opera Theater at the Brattle Theater in Cambridge.

Merrill had the ability to generate theatrical gaiety as proven by *La Perichole*, and the one new offering, *Die Fledermaus*, was one that did bubble.

Merrill and Buckley strengthened casting with a returning John Alexander, and names new to Central City included the much admired Judith Raskin, along with Chester Ludgin, and returning favorites Eva Likova, Clifford Harvuot, Paul Franke, and David Lloyd. David Grusin was the ballet rehearsal pianist, a talent from Littleton, Colorado, who was to go on to fame and fortune with his music for films and TV.

O'Hearn showed he knew how to work a stage, setting up a Viennese park which whirled about to disclose Eisenstein's residence, and at the ball, a red and gold pavilion opened up into a creamy, rococo ballroom. This was theatrical magic of surprising effectiveness, the kind that would dazzle audiences during the five years of Merrill-O'Hearn productions.

A fussy, overlong book interfered with the froth that should make *Die Fledermaus* exuberant, and Buckley was not at his best in striving for airy Viennese flavor.

In reproducing *The Ballad of Baby Doe*, Merrill was feeling his way around this first of many revivals. He was not altogether secure, most noticeably in the final scene on stage at the Tabor Grand Opera House where he placed Tabor in front of the scrim. This broke his relationship with his past, removing him from dreams which should have been very real to him, as in the initial production.

Frank Guarrera delivered an Italianate Tabor, somewhat undone by overfastidious makeup. Laurel Hurley was a lovely Baby Doe, vastly better than the two singers of the opening production. Judith Raskin alternated as Baby Doe, and Mary McMurray alternated as Augusta with Martha Lipton, the one singer from the original production.

The 1959 play, Alex Coppel's *The Gazebo*, with Tom Ewell, was of very thin substance, a long way from the heights reached with *The Lark* or *The Play's The Thing*.

Despite good houses both operas lost money, with a deficit of $57,289 being reported. The season was now being paid for both by ticket sales and a campaign to raise what else might be required, which was not so different from the policy Anne Evans had established years earlier.

At the annual meeting in 1959 it was announced that in 1961 an original work "indigenous to our Rocky Mountain Region" might be done, as this was a "prime function of the Association." It would be 1964 before an original work would be done.

For 1960 an impressive challenge would be served up by two of the most popular operas in the repertory, *Aida* and *Lucia di Lammermoor*.

A Denver architect on the Board, Roger Mead, told Ricketson, "Here's where you stub your toe," but Ricketson always boasted that *Aida* was "the finest ever done without animals."

The manner in which each opera was so triumphantly produced made this a summer to treasure. The major difference was the care given by Merrill to the inumerable details, with O'Hearn a consummate workman and designer. Together they gave new visual style to the productions.

Merrill was notable for being the first American to reach the top ranks of Metropolitan stage directors. His background was Dartmouth, Boston University, the New England Conservatory of Music, and Tanglewood, where like everyone else, he worked with Boris Goldowsky.

Until he went as apprentice director to the Hamburg Opera his work was entirely American, but his talents soon made him an assistant director. Later he went to the Hessian State Opera at Wiesbaden, and subsequently worked at Salzburg and Glyndebourne, and in 1955 joined The Met.

At The Met, Merrill worked with the great singers of the late fifties and sixties. In those days The Met had a category of "Productions Staged By" which consisted of Tyrone Guthrie, Margaret Webster, Herbert Graf, and Cyril Ritchard, and the baby of them all, Nathaniel Merrill.

In the other category of "Stage Directors" Merrill was the only one to rise into the supreme category, those who got to choose cast, conductor, and designer.

At Central City, Merrill found Ricketson and the Board open to new ideas, and in his Central City experience Merrill made many novel approaches to the traditional repertory. His thinking teemed with ways to make opera more vital through movement and design.

When singers as responsive as Beverly Bower, Marguerite Gignac, and Judith Raskin were involved, very fresh results took place. When things did not work out, as with a miscast Beverly Sills as Aida or Dorothy Warenskjold as Violetta, it was because at the time these artists had not matured as stage performers. In any case the wrong role is always to be regretted. And Buckley's musical taste in casting, in which it seemed he had the upper hand, was not always secure.

Merrill and O'Hearn drew strongly on their imaginations for both Verdi and Donizetti in 1960. Merrill went to the picturesque stone wall at the rear of the stage to find more space than had been used for palaces and temples for *Aida* and used the actual back wall for the great hall of the Lammermoors.

In Act I of *Aida* the Palace of the Pharaoh changed before audience eyes to the Temple of Phtha, while in Act II the apartments of Amneris similarly shifted to be replaced by the court of the palace for the triumphal entry. Central City had never seen such dazzling theatrical stagecraft.

Beverly Sills has told how she thought she was going to be singing Lucia at Central City. Aida was not really ever in her voice, certainly not at that early stage of her career, and it never again figured in her repertoire. In later years her Violetta would be affecting Verdi, but Aida was a different kettle of Verdi.

It was Maria Ferriero who had the triumph as Aida, displaying an honest dramatic soprano with a wide-ranging musical, sensitive voice that frequently touched the peaks of operatic art.

Rosalind Elias was vocally lustrous as Amneris but was maladroit dramatically. Joann Grillo excited attention with her first Amneris, introducing opulent singing and sensitive acting.

There were problems with both Rhadames. William Olvis promised a virile tenor but he ran into health problems and retired in favor of the weak Eddy Ruhl, late of the San Carlos Opera. Charles O'Neill was very tall and handsome but had little lift to his tenor.

*Lucia di Lammermoor* was the winner in 1960, achieving a fine blend of drama and vocal quality. It was visually stunning though it did not rely on revolving stages. Donizetti, like Mozart and Rossini, is one for whom this opera house was built, as had been made certain in the 1950 *Don Pasquale*. In this house his music is in an ideal circumstance.

O'Hearn designed lovingly, with a fountain amidst a glen for the lovers' meeting. In the great hall scene, the stage looked larger than ever, standing as an all-time achievement in design. Merrill handled the chorus with dramatic effect.

Casting for *Lucia* was remarkably good, with young singers who responded affectingly to Merrill's coaching. As Adele in *Die Fledermaus*, Judith Raskin had shown a dazzling comic style. Now as Lucia she showed a dark dramatic side, acting with restraint and conviction, thrilling with her silvery soprano.

Marguerite Gignac was altogether astonishing in her dramatic portrayal and her vocal assurance. Her mad scene was one to relish. A French-Canadian singer, she had studied with the mistress of bel canto coloratura, Lina Pagliughli. In but two roles at Central City, the 1960 *Lucia* and the 1961 *Elixir of Love*, she embraced what turned out to be almost her entire operatic career. In 1962 with the San Francisco Opera on tour in Los Angeles she sang Abigaille in Verdi's *Nabucco*, a cruel role in a vast barn where she may have been out of her element. Nothing further was ever heard of her.

John Alexander, one of the best tenors ever at Central City, returned for a richly voiced Edgardo. His alternate was the promising young and handsome Frank Porretta whose career was not much longer than Gignac's. He damaged his voice in a stage production that required much speaking. Other voices to taste in this production were William Wildermann, Joshua Hecht, John Macurdy, Chester Ludgin, and Philip Maero, a very distinguished lot.

Both of these productions seemed to work well for conductor Buckley, and Roger Dexter Fee had the chorus in good stead. It was a Festival to remember.

With *A Thurber Carnival*, for which humorist James Thurber came to Central City, there were further, if contrasting delights. A bright cast including Paul Ford, Peggy Cass, Eddie Mayhoff, and John McGiver, all from the New York edition, made this great entertainment.

Choosing the operas for 1961 was at least half as easy as it usually was because Merrill and O'Hearn were doing their first joint production at The Met, and it would be Donizetti's *The Elixir of Love*. Merrill and Buckley agreed that Marguerite Gignac would be perfectly cast as Adina.

It had been 15 years since *La Traviata* had been done, and as this 1961 season was being called a 30th anniversary, it made a fitting choice.

In an interview in *The New York Times* O'Hearn explained how he built his designs for *The Elixir* around a grape arbor motif. "I've made up my own village, grape arbors, vertical buildings broken up by balconies, windows and lattices, hills in the distance."

On this same occasion O'Hearn dissociated himself from heavy stylization, and pointed out that Merrill "whom he admires greatly as a technical director, was always full of ideas about scenery and costumes. . . . . . There was a constant exchange of ideas about such things as floor plans and stage business."

*La Traviata* opened the season with a production I described as "a case of magnificent scenery looking for singers to match." O'Hearn designed an opening scene with the vast underside of a giant staircase that startled viewers. The pretty voice of the popular radio star Dorothy Warenskjold failed to locate the pathos of Violetta. With little experience, the diminutive Hawaiian tenor Charles L.K. Davis projected neither vocally nor dramatically. Central City's Mr. Reliable, Clifford Harvuot, delivered a warm, positive elder Germont.

*The Elixir of Love* was turned out with the finest theatrical magic its production staff could achieve. The casting was as good for Donizetti as it had been weak for Verdi. Buckley led an ebullient performance. It was another production to cherish.

Marguerite Gignac dazzled audiences with her blithe coloratura, while the alternating Adina, Mildred Allen, was certainly winsome in spite of lacking a true coloratura. There were two notable Nemorinos, the fine tenors John Alexander and David Lloyd, with Alexander offering the more vocal riches and Lloyd the finer agility.

As Belcaro, Frank Guarrera was made up to look like Cantinflas, the Mexican comic, but although he had done the part at The Met, he was another stumbling baritone when it came to this music. Chester Ludgin cut a dashing figure and sang ably as his alternate. Neither Spiro Malas nor Ralph Herbert was ideal vocally though these were lively Dulacmaras.

William Gibson's stirring *The Miracle Worker* followed, with Eileen Brennan a forceful Annie Sullivan and 12-year old Donna Zimmerman as the gutsy Helen Keller.

Although Puccini was born in 1858 it was decided to honor him in 1962 with a Puccini Festival by presenting *La Boheme* and *The Girl of the Golden West*. Eleanor Steber had done *The Girl* at Red Rocks in 1958, and it had not made much of an impression. A successful San Francisco production in 1965 made waves and now it is in the standard repertory.

At Central City, Merrill and O'Hearn found a dramatic center for the work, and through music, color, and lighting, set a very involving, affecting mood. They made the most of the strongest portion of the opera, its first act, opening on a scrim curtain vista of a small Western mountain town through which the Polka Tavern barroom gradually became visible.

Beverly Bower was a perfect Minnie, fresh-voiced with a welcome vocal opulence, and the control to soften the voice to convey gentler emotions. She was plucky enough to do the required Biblical readings as well as handle her pistol with authority.

Richard Cassily, recently a Wagnerian tenor at The Met and elsewhere, was a strong Dick Johnson, with Robert Moulson vocally promising but stiff in presence as his alternate. Chester Ludgin took on Jack Rance for the dark-hearted man he was, and made a strong impression, while Clifford Harvuot was at his snarling best as the alternating Rance.

A strong male cast included Herbert Beattie as Jake Wallace, with Spiro Malas his weak alternate. John Macurdy, Robert Trehy, Norman Kelley, Norman Scott, and Benjamin Rayson filled out the cast with virility and exciting sound. Lynn Owen was a disturbingly pallid alternate Minnie.

It had now been ten years since *La Boheme* had been done, and it was worth waiting for. O'Hearn's major departure from tradition was in Act I where a stairwell slightly off center stage for entrances as well as Benoit's hasty departure brought the of action front and center.

Strong casting made the emotions ring. Mildred Allen here was in her proper element, a sensitive Puccini artist, while the alternating Mimi was the auspicious Arlene Saunders. By now John Alexander had arrived at The Met and had new assurance. He had a triumph as Rodolpho. David Lloyd was again his alternate, a lyrical, admirable singer. There were Marcellos by Chester Ludgin, Clifford Harvuot, and Benjamin Rayson, and Norman Scott was an imposing Colline. Robert Trehy and William Beck alternated as Schaunard.

Ronald Eyer of *The New York Herald-Tribune* was particularly impressed with *The Girl of the Golden West* which he wrote, was brought "alive in a remarkably convincing way," going on to say that "the Central City producers do nothing revolutionary in the staging of the operas by way of avant-garde or experimental methods. Their ways are the traditional ones with a fine bead on detailed realism."

Eyer raised the question, "When are our American singers going to learn to sing English as well as they normally sing foreign languages?" He found that "barely 20 per cent of the words were intelligible." From the start Central City had done all operas in English language translations. This was a keystone of its operation. Standards of singing English intelligibly have improved much over the years.

Jean Kerr's merry *Mary, Mary* was smartly performed by a cast led by Patricia Smith and Lee Bowman, shrewdly directed by Joseph Anthony, who had also directed the memorable *The Lark*.

When it was announced that the 1963 Central City bill would be Mozart's *Don Giovanni* and Verdi's *Il Trovatore*, both in debut productions, it struck some as rather too much vengeful swordsplay without the leavening of good spirits and wit one usually hoped to encounter at Central City.

This daunting bill drew some of Merrill and O'Hearn's strongest work. For *Don Giovanni*, O'Hearn delivered one of his most appealing and imaginative designs. Its raked stage, with balconies surmounted by a great crowning canopy, worked splendidly, while transparent scrims towards the rear of the stage suggested golden corridors stretching into infinity. The entire stage was taken over for the great hall of the final scene.

Merrill raised the curtain for the overture, during which the statue of the Commendatore was the focus of attention. An opera with many lengthy arias, it needed a strong visual sense, which Merrill and O'Hearn were prepared to deliver. O'Hearn triggered gaily colored streamers to fall prior to the ball scene. A fine looking cast, imaginative sets, and dramatic lighting provided much for the eye to feast upon.

In the ideal proportions of the Central City Opera House, Merrill developed relationships so that the drama took on an intimate quality. Buckley prepared a stronger than usual orchestra, utilizing the Prague version, which meant, regrettably, losing Ottavio's "Dalla sua pace" and Elvira's "Mi tradi," two highlights of the score. But the opera moved right along.

At this time in his career Norman Treigle was about to crest when with Beverly Sills he would bring new distinction to the New York City Opera with the widely praised production of Handel's *Julius Caesar*. Treigle's Mephistopheles in Boito's opera was hailed as exceptional. His dashing 1956 Mozart Figaro for the Greater Denver Metropolitan Opera had indicated the kind of singing actor he was to become.

His Don was a lithe, sardonic character of great vigor, commanding attention with the strength of his style, and the force and nuance of his singing.

There was a special flourish in Merrill's stage direction with its emphasis on the dualism of man as personified in the Don and in Leporello, with Herbert Beattie relishing his role in the proceedings.

Beverly Bower returned for a lustrous Donna Anna. It was no replay of her Minnie. Mary Ellen Pracht was attractive and a good deal more than competent as Elvira while Mary Jennings, a Miss Arkansas and Metropolitan Opera finalist, charmed as Zerlina.

In his first major operatic role, Sherrill Milnes was a stalwart Masetto, showing great promise, while Justino Diaz made an early appearance as the Commendatore. Mallory Walker brought verve to Ottavio.

In the alternating cast, Richard Cross displayed a fine baritone and Spiro Malas was a nimble Leporello. They did not strike fire as had Treigle and Beattie.

The fine singing actress Eileen Schauler was Bower's equal in vocal intelligence but her own vulnerable persona. Marguerite Willauer handled Elvira capably and Ginetta La Bianca, an experienced singer, was a winning Zerlina. William Beck did a good Masetto and Thomas Paul was imposing as the Commendatore.

Things were changing. In this production Charles Anthony was the lone representative from The Met. He had made his Met debut in 1954, changing his name to Anthony from his real name, Caruso, as he did so. His was a routine Ottavio. Anthony in 1993 was nearing his 40th anniversary at The Met.

In the chorus of this production were such illustrious singers as Samuel Ramey, who has since attested to the stimulus this experience gave to his career; Edward Sooter, Wagnerian tenor, and Carolyne James, who returned in 1978 for a chilling Madame Flora in *The Medium*, and has frequently sung at the Santa Fe Opera, even as she chose to change her name to Clarity James.

So great were the demands for *Don Giovanni* that no dual casting was shared with the other opera in the repertory, Verdi's *Il Trovatore* which had its own heavy requirements. Bernard Stambler, who worked so well with Robert Ward in the exceptional adaptation of Arthur Miller's *The Crucible*, did the English version, as well as making a decision to present the opera as *The Trobador* in the antique Provencal spelling, rather than in the accepted Italian.

For the first time since her 1956 Tosca, Lucine Amara was back at Central City, singing with assured vocal velvet, but no more than ever interested in the theatrical aspects of opera. It was her alternate Maria Ferriero, always expressive and intense who galvanized the audience. She was another performer of great promise who seemed to vanish from sight. She had done the Countess in the Richard Strauss *Capriccio* at Santa Fe, the Aida at Central City, and this Leonora, and then she vanished.

Richard Cassily as Manrico looked like an Irish gypsy but gave little pleasure with his dry voice and pitch problems. There was little dramatic impact in John Craig's sweet tenor sound.

In a characterization of amazing physical intensity, Joann Grillo was a terrific Azucena. Margaret Roggero was from the clutch-and-swagger school, and her singing was overly cautious. Chester Ludgin was a striking Count di Luna, his singing bringing as much excitement as his acting, while Benjamin Rayson gave a fine resonance to his alternate count.

This production would be the last by Nathaniel Merrill at Central City until his 1972 return. Distinctive as his productions had been, largely critical successes and well attended, they were costly. The 1963 costs with their separate casting were $193,706, of which salaries were $32,890, which seems small. Sets cost $17,890. Ticket sales were large at $143,687, but with overhead, there was an awesome loss of $118,964.

For Merrill, the 60s would be increasingly demanding of his time at The Met. With production requirements at Central City increasing under the new Ford Foundation grant program, it was understandable though regrettable that this important Merrill phase was ending.

# THE FORD FOUNDATION AND A LADY

In 1961, the Ford Foundation initiated a national program to encourage development of administrative and managerial personnel for theaters, opera companies, and symphony orchestras. In 1963 Central City was granted $35,000 annually for a five-year period to begin in 1965.

In this time sequence, the Association would add a third production for a minimum of eight performances in 1965, and in 1966 the Association would raise $17,500 to match one-half of the grant, and by 1968 would raise another $17,500. For Central City to add another, third, production would always be difficult because of the limitations of the house seating, a constraining factor in meeting expenses.

Ever since the success of *Baby Doe* Ricketson had been trying to find another Colorado opera, and at the annual meeting there was reiteration of the old song-and-dance about doing *Kiss Me Kate*, *Carousel*, or *The Beggar's Opera*.

Among the various plaques by the Opera Garden, between the opera house and the Teller House, there is a plaque which reads as follows:

> *World's Premiere*
> *"The Lady from Colorado"*
> *Robert Ward, Composer*
> *Bernard Stambler*
>
> *Librettis Emerson Buckley*
>
> *Conductor*
> *From Homer Croy's Novel.*
> *Friday, July 3, 1964*

Readers should recognize that Stambler was indeed the librettist, and that Librettis was not really a part of conductor Buckley's name.

Homer Croy's book for *The Lady From Colorado* told the story of Katie Lawder, an Irish girl who in the late 1880s married Cecil Moon, an English remittance man with great land holdings near Fort Collins. When he inherited his title she became Lady Moon. It was this story which absorbed millions of radio listeners as *My Gal Sunday*. Croy's book had almost no conflict, and Stambler attempted to impose some melodrama on it but it did not work.

Rick was attracted by the idea of a light-hearted musical, and a big budget was settled on the production, which the old hand Oenslager would design. A new hand, Christopher West, director of opera theater at Juilliard School of Music, was hired to stage the opera and also *Madama Butterfly*.

Patton Campbell, Oenslager's assistant on *Baby Doe* costumes, returned to do enchanting 1886 costumes, and the admired dancer-choreographer, Helen Tamiris, came in to do some dances.

A large cast was needed to populate the mythical Colorado town of Elkhorn and the splashy final scene at the Brown Palace Hotel. Pretty Mary Ellen Pracht was Katie with the charming Davis Cunningham as dashing Cecil Moon. Mary Jennings was a glowing beauty with Thomas Hayward in the alternate cast.

In very slight roles were such fine singers as Mignon Dunn, Chester Ludgin, Herbert Beattie, Thomas Paul, and more good voices as alternates, Raymond Michaelski, Spiro Malas, Marcia Baldwin, and John Fiorito. Beattie's role was a steal from Charles Laughton's *Ruggles of Red Gap* as a British butler on the frontier. Among those in the chorus was David Holloway who in 1984 would be a Rigoletto and in 1988 a Macbeth at Central City.

The flawed libretto was too novelistic for effective dramatic treatment, with sentimentalized rather than lightly satirized characters. There was not much inventiveness to the stock dramatic devices which were used to propel the story.

Ward's musical skills produced some pleasing melodies but nothing ever happened in the music, which became earthbound in the second act.

In The New York Times, Ross Parmenter wrote that "although gold is still being found in Central City, the Association hasn't found the same lode in *The Lady from Colorado* that it did in *Baby Doe*. Lady is nearly all corn. Its chief characters are stereotypes. And the music, far from having the naivite of genuine innocence, has the professionalism of opera composers turning their hands to a *Paint Your Wagon* type Broadway show."

In The *Cleveland Press* Frank Hruby wrote that "the story, none too strong to begin with, seems to abound in non-sequiturs and unmotivated situations - a colorful razzle-dazzle spectacle of which they may be justly proud."

The demands of *Lady* were so great that director West had to pull *Madama Butterfly* together in a hurry, and it showed. Oenslager had failed to apply his usually fine perspective to its sets which seemed cluttered and crude. Beverly Bower did not have another success. Cio-Cio-San was another lady in every sense, and was not for her.

The climax of West's stage direction was the death scene, as a self-conscious Butterfly flapped her arms in shadow play. John Craig's smooth tenor pleased though he lacked conviction as Pinkerton.

This Festival had its share of grief, for Christopher West had been critically ill during the preparation phases and died in the autumn of 1965, while Helen Tamiris was forced to depart because of the deterioration of her health, and she died in the same year.

For 1964 expenses were high at $208,613. Ticket income was $147,312, higher than in 1963, but within a few hundred dollars of being the same as 1962. The large sum of $119,964 had to be raised.

One of the brightest comedies in a long time, Neil Simon's *Barefoot in the Park*, was a delightful finale, and with Myrna Loy exuding old-time glamour there was class to be seen. Joan van Ark, the young Boulder actress, was in her first major role, and showed her kind of class, the kind that would keep her popular into the 90s when she continued to perform in television's *Knot's Landing*. Richard Benjamin, later to become a film director, was the juvenile lead.

Ricketson would have preferred to leave his presidency on a brighter note, with *Lady* as a great triumph but its general failure was sobering to a man of such jaunty disposition.

After Ricketson, the Association would find itself in the turmoil of efforts to find a capable producer-director. Those other struggles to weather the severe economic jolts that made opera so costly and the need to find just where Central City stood in the changing tastes of the day took their toll.

As he had done many times in different guise, Ricketson advised the Board, "The goal of yesterday will be the starting point of tomorrow."

# TRAVAILS

The first year of the five-year Ford Foundation grant marked the onset of uneasy times. Some Board members had the idea that the grant was a Lorelei, beckoning them onto the rocks of financial ruin. The problem of meeting the expenses of an expanded season was better comprehended by the Association than by the Foundation.

The initial Ford Foundation grant came on October 1, 1964, and it was $35,000 of a $175,000 package. The budget for 1965, the first year in which three operas would be done, was $243,024, with salaries increased to $130,424. That $35,000 would not go far. Don Carney, a banker who had come on as President, Ricketson, now Chairman of the Board, and the Board had full plates before them.

Rainy weather struck, and there were times when audiences could not reach Central City. The stream beneath the stage became swollen from the rains, endangering the house. When the Association asked special funds from the Foundation to compensate for several canceled performances, they were turned down.

The budget was a shoestring budget, for the Foundation was not giving enough to make a real difference, in the face of doing three operas. The Foundation, for its part, aimed at strengthening the future of opera, but the Association was concerned that the effort to stage three productions over a five-week period might be too demanding of the available forces, with insufficient time for musical and dramatic preparation.

The relationship between the Association and the Foundation was never an easy one, and it was very nearly severed when the D'Oyly Carte Company was signed for a 1968 program anticipated to resolve financial worries. This would be the fourth year of the grant. When 1968 came around, there was no $35,000 check from the Foundation.

In 1965, the initial year of the grant, three operas were produced. Massenet's *Manon* and Delibes's *Lakme* were being done for the first time, continuing the expansion of repertory, while Rossini's *The Barber of Seville* had not been done since 1941.

The combination was heady, with French lyrical drama, French exotic melodrama, and opera buffa elbowing each other for attention. While there was merit to the idea of selecting operas in which basic casting could be shared, it was loosely applied in the actual casting.

A new production team was on hand, led by John Brownlee, the much-admired baritone from The Met and Glyndebourne and Figaro of the 1941 *Barber* as stage director, with Jean-Claude Rinfret from Montreal as stage designer. Buckley was there, observing his tenth year as conductor.

*Manon* was the most ambitious of the efforts. In Rinfret's costly, overrealistic, and highly detailed designs, the opera looked expensive. Elaine Malbin led the opening night cast as Manon, with vocal intensity and dark beauty to spare, while as Des Grieux, Stanley Kolk brought a stalwart appearance and a sweet, firm tenor. There was perfectly good casting with Dominic Cossa, Arnold Voketaitis, and Howard Fried standing out. Somehow there was a lack of emotional conviction in the performance which stemmed from stilted acting, a response to Brownlee's efforts to impart style, and a less than subtle English adaptation.

The chorus lacked the individualization of its members usually seen on this stage, and in the orchestra there was a lack of idiomatic playing. Alternate Mary Jennings was as much a beauty as ever but was wanting in vocal style and projection. Clifford Harvuot and Russell Christopher were strong in support but Gene Bullard was an inadequate Des Grieux.

The Lakmes were Patricia Brooks, Ginetta La Bianca, and Nadja Witkowska, and the balance of the cast was basically that of *Manon*. The faded exoticism of this opera seemed not to belong at Central City, and it was ordinarily executed, a poorly done travel brochure for Kashmir.

*The Barber of Seville* enjoyed Chester Ludgin's bumptious Figaro and Patricia Brooks sparkling Rosina, as well as Herbert Beattie's fine Dr. Bartolo, but Brownlee's staging was square, lacking the individuality and style of his own performing. Rinfret's sets looked flimsy.

Robert C. Marsh wrote in *Musical America* of his admiration for Herbert Beattie's Bartolo, which struck him as being "the finest Bartolo I have encountered in some time, and in the light of what I had seen him do earlier this year in San Francisco, I was again impressed by the sensitivity and range of this young singing actor."

Marsh thought there was too much forced vocal production in *Manon*, and that *Lakme* "deals with stereotyped characters and invites stereotyped characterization."

*Any Wednesday* was comedy of little consequence, and other than the presences of Loretta Swit, who would later adorn TV's MASH, and of George Gaynes, the Hungarian-born opera singer in an acting role, there was little to report.

For 1965 a tenth anniversary production of *The Ballad of Baby Doe* was planned, along with *Carmen* and *The Italian Girl in Algiers*. Christopher West was set to direct, and Donald Oenslager would return for his first full season since 1948, with *Baby Doe* in revival and two new productions.

West's death late in 1965 made it necessary to replace him, and James Lucas turned out to be the new man. As a junior in college he had staged *Carmen* but *Baby Doe* and *The Italian Girl in Algiers* were new to him. His background was primarily academic, opera at Tanglewood and Juilliard with students.

At this time the Rossini comedy was infrequently performed so was a true novelty. This rich serving of Turkish delight was topped off by Buckley who served up a sparkling performance of Rossini's music in all its Venetian vivacity. It was the triumph the new team sought.

Lucas found a satirical spirit, working for enlivening details for principals and chorus. Herbert Beattie was magnificently roguish as Mustafa, impressing with his well-blended singing and acting. Marcia Baldwin was a vivacious, sure Isabella, Stanley Kolk was in spirited form, and William Beck was a lively Taddeo.

In the alternate cast Corrine Curry delighted with the ease of her singing and her presence as Isabella, while tenor William Dembaugh ran into problems in the high range. Lee Cass as Mustafa overdid the physical comedy.

*Carmen* called for special attention in an effort to correct the flaws of the 1954 production. Although the setting was not intended as a unit set, it remained basic in each of the four acts. Working best in Acts I and II, it seemed stretched for the mountain hideaway of Act III. In the final scene, a fountain at stage center got in the way of dramatic logic, because Carmen could have easily evaded Don Jose by running around it. There were cheers for Act II with the moonlight filtering through the tavern skylight.

There was drama in the look of this Oenslager *Carmen*, with what seemed to be a road of destiny going through its scenes with earthy browns, reds, and yellows in perspectives which made the stage seem large rather than diminished in the manner of the 1954 production.

Buckley believed the opera ran too long, so omitted the preludes to Acts II and III, but an unusually large compliment of Denver Symphony Orchestra musicians improved the quality of the orchestra. Among members of the chorus were baritone Lenus Carlson and soprano Janice Yoes who went on to strong careers.

Joann Grillo was a sure, powerful Carmen, controlled in her playing. Her Don Jose was Thomas Hayward, always musically reliable, but his pudgy shape and the absence of edge in his acting proved laugh-provoking in scenes of intense drama. Chester Ludgin had a strong grip on Escamillo and Mary Jennings in blonde pigtails was an appealing Micaela.

Tempestuous June Genovese used the velvet of her mezzo and highly emotional playing to make vivid drama. Richard Kness, Joann Grillo's new husband, made his operatic debut as Don Jose. His virile presence offset the tentative character of his singing. Since then he has sung at The Met, while Joann Grillo sang there through the 1987-88 season.

Frank Guarrera's alternating Escamillo had stylish demeanor but he was troubled by the high register of the role. June Card was a pretty Micaela with lovely tone, and much was expected of her at the time. Later she emerged in Europe where she has had a successful career.

Among those doing small roles were Michael Devlin, Leo Goeke, Thomas Palmer, and Beverly Evans, all of whom have gone on to prime careers.

Again *The Ballad of Baby Doe* was immensely popular, and again it was dominated by the superlative Augusta of Frances Bible, originator of this role. Frank Guarrera repeated his 1959 Tabor, with stronger impact this time. Chester Ludgin took a turn as Tabor with dramatic force. The Baby Does of Nadja Witkowska and Lucille Kailer were unexciting.

One Neil Simon comedy leads to another, so it was no surprise that the TV comic George Gobel would come to Central City for *The Odd Couple*, a great success.

For 1967 Oenslager again designed three new productions with James Lucas back as stage director. The productions would be Verdi's grand opera, *A Masked Ball*, Lehar's *The Merry Widow*, back for the first time since 1933, and that all-time favorite, *Don Pasquale*, a strong bill.

Oenslager designed *The Merry Widow* for opulence, with elaborate costuming by Suzanne Mess. Lucas used Christopher Hassell's London version, revised by Milton Lazarus with new lyrics by Forman Brown. The book was constantly being broken up by ill-conceived efforts to update the material, and Lucas lacked decisiveness in what should be retained or eliminated.

Mary Jennings in her sixth year at Central City was Sonia, as the Hanna of this version was called, and she turned a cartwheel and elsewhere radiated charm. Her Danilo was the roguish David Smith, while Harry Theyard was on the threshold of a major career. He brought a fine lilt to Camille's music.

In the alternating cast, Elizabeth Cole was skilled but uningratiating as Sonia, while Nolan Van Way was both dapper and resonant as Danilo. William Dembaugh was back with his lack of presence and vocal problems.

There were delightful singers like Norman Kelley, sheerly professional as Popoff, while James Billings was an Otto Soglow cartoon as Nish. Potentials were shown by Michael Devlin and Malcolm Smith.

In the end, this was simply too much Broadway and not enough of European charm despite Oenslager's sumptuous sets.

Central City's ambitions for *A Masked Ball* needed to be of sterner stuff. Its outsized Verdi passions crowded the opera house.

With Richard Kness breaking his ankle and Malcolm Smith hurting his ankle seriously in a fall, there were odds against getting this opera on stage.

Among the number of fine voices were Eileen Schauler whose intelligence and sensitivity made her Amelia winning, and Benjamin Rayson was resonant as Ankerstrom. Richard Kness brought excitement as King Gustave, for this production provided the rarely used Swedish setting Verdi had hoped for, before the censors got to his opera.

Buckley brought along Gianni Savelli, the Kansan who turned his name into an Italian one, and pushed for what he thought was a brilliant Italian sound, but it came off as tasteless, reminding one of the comic Jerry Colonna with his frantic operatic spoofs.

Then there was Athena Lampropoulos, a Greek import, who it was hoped might turn out to be another Maria Callas, but her eccentric singing, her large unruly voice, left much to be done. After a few performances at the New York City Opera she vanished from the scene.

Oenslager's sets were big, ranging from palace to gallow's field, and to the splendor of the ball itself. They were massive, and did not move as had O'Hearn's for *Aida*. Lucas failed to bring focus to the drama.

*Don Pasquale* was a tour de force for Herbert Beattie in his richly characterized Don. Oenslager, having given his all to the Lehar and Verdi productions, came up with drab sets with paint spots visible on opening night. James Lucas directed for physical comedy but Beattie worked to minimize this. Joy Clements was fetchingly pretty as Norina and sang charmingly while alternate June Card used her voice well but seemed detached. There were tenor troubles in spades with two inadequate Ernestos.

Fun of a sophisticated sort came in Abe Burrows' farcical *Cactus Flower* which featured TV's popular star of *Gunsmoke*, Hugh O'Brian, with the lovely Elizabeth Allen.

Curiously, when it had been earlier established that the D'Oyly Carte Opera Company would play a five-week season in 1968, there was an announcement in the midst of the 1967 Festival that *Rigoletto*, Bizet's *The Pearl Fishers*, and Robert Ward's *The Crucible* would be done in 1968 with Buckley returning as musical director.

Towering expenses of $317,124 with ticket sales of $192,867, a new record in sales, were reported but the long season led to a $211,158 loss. In the face of this, the temptation to do a D'Oyly Carte season was irresistible.

But it was not going to be easy. At the end of the 1967 season, the contracts between the American Guild of Musical Artists, known as AGMA, and the Association had expired, and AGMA was determined to improve the singers' financial situation. Dropping the D'Oyly Carte season into this mix was hardly going to ease the situation, for AGMA now worked to restore the Verdi, Bizet, and Robert Ward season.

The Association claimed the demands to be excessive, and that no operas at all would be performed if AGMA continued to press its case. In England, British Equity supported the AGMA position, that American singers should be performing in Central City.

In February, *Variety* reported that D'Oyly Carte would cancel its season rather than become involved in the international union problems. A parenthetical note in *Variety* observed that "Central City is very much an adjunct of the social season of Denver's elite."

Somehow the D'Oyly Carte threat to cancel was not brought to the attention of the Association. However, it was aware of the web of complications that had been created. During the summer when not involved in *Don Pasquale*, Herbert Beattie had been working to renegotiate the AGMA contract. In an interview with *The Denver Post*, Beattie indicated that the Association might have been working illegally, saying "you don't do that - you can't negotiate with a union about an opera contract, and then engage another company."

D'Oyly Carte was in an untenable position with the Association threatening to stay dark unless Gilbert and Sullivan were allowed, while British Equity was for strong union recognition.

On February 24, 1968, the Association sent the following telegram to both D'Oyly Carte and AGMA: "Resolved that unless AGMA immediately ceases its action to prevent the appearance of D'Oyly Carte at Central City in 1968, the Association allow D'Oyly Carte to withdraw from its contract, and the Association refrain from presenting opera at Central City during the season of 1968."

The Association in the course of this brouhaha made the claim that more than $1 million had been lost in doing opera. It was fortunate that Anne Evans was not there to make the blistering comment that would have been likely.

On March 23, By Faine, AGMA national executive secretary, and singer Norman Kelley, an AGMA Board member, and Association representatives William McGlone, Bruce Alexander, and Ricketson met in Denver. A week later it was announced that the D'Oyly Carte engagement would take place as scheduled, and that in 1969 and 1970 opera would return, though other aspects of the new contract that made this possible were not detailed. At any rate, increases for AGMA artists and certain staff members would be made.

With the altering of the agreement with the Ford Foundation, there was no 1968 grant forthcoming. In the final year of this grant, a loss of $222,750 stood as the difference between income and expense.

The Gilbert and Sullivan season began June 22 with *The Mikado*, with advance tickets at a record high. Over $140,000 had been paid the visiting troupe, and by the end of the operetta season, ticket sales had reached a high of $217,012. In turn there were *H.M.S. Pinafore, Yeoman of Guard, The Pirates of Penzance, The Mikado,* and *Iolanthe*.

John Reed became the hero of this season, with his Ko-Ko, Jack Point, Lord Chancellor, Major-General, and Sir Joseph Porter. In the 1955 engagement, Reed was a chorus member, and in the meantime had brushed his style with the special brand of wit and foolishness needed for these mostly jovial personages. Starting in 1981, Reed became the producer of an annual G & S Festival at the University of Colorado in Boulder, and it has become an integral part of the Colorado summer entertainment scene.

As successful as the season had been, there was no such luck in the weak play offering, Terence Fisby's *There's a Girl in My Soup* with Don Ameche and Taina Elg. It did notably poor business, and led to inter-executive wrangling between Ricketson and publicist Robert Lotito, reported in the press.

It was clear that opera would be back in Central City in 1969 when *Tosca* and *Die Fledermaus* would be done. James Lucas returned as stage director and Klaus Holm, son of choreographer and *Baby Doe* director Hanya Holm, and former lighting assistant to Oenslager, would design the productions. Costumes were rented from the New York City Opera. This would be Buckley's final full season at Central City, his thirteenth.

Eileen Schauler gave a splendid, spellbinding Tosca, marked by admirable musicality. Benjamin Rayson's work showed growth in a Scarpia that had bite. Robert Moulson was in fresh, full voice as Cavaradossi.

Marisa Galvany's alternating Tosca was not up to the role, and her performance never got off the ground. Gianna Savelli was back as the alternating Cavaradossi to hurl his tenor about. Theodore Lambrinos was a small-scaled Scarpia. Klaus Holm's sets were overly traditional without appeal.

*Die Fledermaus* included champagne gags, costume gags, singing gags, orchestra gags, and Central City gags, all stupefying and rarely funny. Buckley didn't have his Viennese tempos in gear, and things didn't mesh.

Mary Jennings, despite her dreadful ball gown, sparkled as the opening night Rosalinda, while Louisa De Set was a pert Adele, singing with a tone richer than that of the usual Adele. Dominic Cossa was an affable Falke with Dan Marek a dull Eisenstein. Gene Bullard amused with his impudent Alfredo. For a change, Prince Orlovsky was done not by a female but by Jack Harrold who romped outrageously. James Billings as Frosch was a bit too obviously a Broadway comic.

In her fourth season at Central City, Nadja Witkowska was a lustrous, bemused Rosalinda, wearing her own version of Leo Van Witsen's ugly ball gown. In this cast Nico Castel was a suave Eisenstein, with a spirited Alfredo by Gary Glaze. William Beck was the Falke in this cast.

Howard Keel, the popular film baritone of *Show Boat* and *Kiss Me Kate*, came not to sing but to act three different parts of Neil Simon's 1968 comedy, *Plaza Suite*, smartly directed by Mike Nichols. Keel and Betty Garrett and the play did not draw strong audiences, and this presentation lost $6,640.

With ticket sales of $185,232 there still were losses of $168,000 for this five-week season. The Ford Foundation was back with its $35,000 support. It had not required three operas to be done, as the Association had finally made its point to the Foundation that it just was not feasible to produce a three-opera season without greater support. And that support had not yet been found in Denver.

The purpose of the Ford Foundation grant had been to induce more people to attend opera at Central City by offering more performances. Ticket income in the year prior to the onset of the grant was $143,000 and in its final year, that source of income had gone up by $40,000, so the experiment, perilous as it had been, was successful. It had shown that there was a large potential for audience-building that need to be recognized.

In January 1970 the Association met to hear John Fleming Kelly, chairman of a special review and planning committee, urge the Association to recall the storied past of Central City as they worked to keep pace with the times. Three concrete objectives were given the Association by the Board. These were increased cooperation with other organizations in the promotion of musical performing arts in Colorado; raising about 25% more in Association funds, and formulating recommendations concerning a capital funds program.

In March, announcement was made that *Of Mice and Men* and *La Boheme* would be staged for a five-week festival. There would be 22 performances of the Puccini revival and 18 of the new opera, a new work by Carlisle Floyd, based on Steinbeck's short novel and subsequent play and film.

The Floyd opera had been premiered by the Seattle Opera in January 1970 to universal acclaim, with *Time* calling it "the most moving musical drama to come out of America since the natives of Catfish Row tangled with Porgy and Bess back in 1935." Floyd's *Susannah* had been a success nationally since its 1955 premiere, and in 1958 his *Wuthering Heights* was premiered by the Santa Fe Opera, though it was found to be lacking in romantic sweep.

Central City jumped to acquire the rights and to contract Frank Corsaro, director of the Seattle production, who had been to Central City in 1952 as part of the company doing Mary Chase's *Mrs. McThing*, starring Helen Hayes. Corsaro had lately established a strong reputation for innovative opera productions at the New York City Opera.

Julian Patrick, George of the Seattle production, and Robert Moulson, its Lennie, as well as Carol Bayard, its Curley's Wife, were signed for Central City, with Thomas P. Martin contracted as conductor, with Norman Johnson as assistant conductor, and Klaus Holm to design the sets.

It was thought that *Time's* review would put the mark of success on the *Of Mice and Men* project. Ricketson alone of the Board voted against it, and now later said it was "not a subject for opera at Central City where you need music that is in your heart."

With eighteen performances to sell, and a narrative which some found depressing, there were problems. The idea of a new, downbeat opera kept audiences so small that it played to no more than fifty per cent of capacity.

That frame of reference was represented by one lady who thought "it was just too bad that Verdi hadn't lived to write the music."

*Time* had gone on to write that " Floyd has fleshed out the bleak Steinbeck characters, revealed their loneliness and longing behind their failure, and given them music that raises their foolishness, vanity, and ambition to the level of high tragedy. The music is extraordinarily singable; its effect is that of glowingly lyrical somewhat familiar music that one has never heard before. Floyd's libretto transforms Steinbeck's tragic tale of a misunderstood simpleton into a threnody for lost men haunted by a dream - in this case the dream of a farm of their own."

At the time I wrote that "this is an occasion for which Central City takes great credit honorably." My only criticism was of Holm's excessively literal sets. Both Glenn Giffin of *The Denver Post* and Thomas MacCluskey of the *Rocky Mountain News* were enthusiastic.

With it the Association took the biggest loss ever - $271,000. 18 performances was a severe miscalculation of popular acceptance for an opera of such challenging substance.

Corsaro's *La Boheme* was engagingly non-traditional. Among the innovations were an indoor Cafe Momus, (sensible in view of the outdoor chill of Christmas Eve), Parpignol selling French postcards, Musetta perched like Helen Morgan atop an upright piano, and the introduction of pretty girls for Schaunard's first-act party.

Karen Altman and Mallory Walker fused the production with grace and conviction. Thomas Palmer's sardonic Marcello, William Ledbetter's Schaunard, and Will Roy's Colline were convincing as well as vocally skilled.

Of the other singers I wrote that "Patricia Craig (in the alternate cast) at first appeared to have mixed up her Puccini operas, and was performing with the hauteur and grand manner of Floria Tosca. Her Mimi was not ill; she had an ego problem."

Conductor Martin deferred too much to the singers, which stymied the Puccini orchestral sound.

The accumulated deficit after this season was close to $115,000, with an actual net cash loss of $42,769.

In August, during the successful run of *Forty Carats*, executive director Robert J. Brown submitted his resignation. No less than two days later Carl H.P. Dahlgren, former artist's manager for Sol Hurok, was named executive director.

Dahlgren lost no time in putting his concept of the Central City Festival before the public, something Brown had never done. A month later Dahlgren said "The Opera House belongs not only to Colorado but to the country. It should be regarded with pride, almost like a national heritage which it is."

Dahlgren believed Central City should receive the kind of restoration support the Rockefellers had given for Williamsburg, Virginia, and that talented and "disadvantaged youth" should be given a chance to work at Central City with prominent people from the artistic fields.

When the annual meeting took place in November 1970, the Association was informed that $135,000 would be required to get the red ink under control. Some Board members were frank in urging curtailment of productions for one or two years. Elimination of opera in 1971 was a strong possibility, and Association President Myron Neusteter declared that " it is not the intention of the Association to do away with opera permanently, and we will do opera whenever and wherever possible."

When Dahlgren told the Association that the 1970 cost had exceeded $600,000, and unpaid bills for the Teller House amounted to $33,000, an air of profound sobriety settled in.

Dahlgren saw to it that the Association passed a resolution enabling Central City to become a national monument by 1976, the Centennial Year, and Neusteter was hopeful about the money, saying "we have no problem but financial support."

In the *Rocky Mountain News* Pasquale Marranzino wrote a column pleading with supporters to "save the opera,"continuing "I wish we'd all stand and make with a deafening 'Encore! Encore!'"

Already there were rumors that *The Unsinkable Molly Brown* would be just the thing to bring Central City financial security, while others said opera should continue but be presented in concert style, if a grant could be obtained.

One of the more intriguing bits of business which transpired following the 1970 season was that Oliver Smith, noted scenic designer of *Oklahoma, Guys* and *Dolls*, and the ballet *Rodeo*, and co-chairman of American Ballet Theater, proposed to the Board that he serve it as Artistic Advisor, urging a shift from operas and theater to opera and good music for the entire summer season.

For 1971 he proposed a Bernstein Festival, urging a rise in artistic quality, and these he thought would make the Festival internationally famous.

In the minutes of the Executive Committee it was noted that someone observed the Smith "seems to see Central City as a place to build a monument to himself."

As early as June 1970, before the Festival opened, *The Denver Post* editorialized that "we believe" Central City deserves special support not only because of its high quality but also because (1) it has undertaken a thorough program of self-evaluation and organizational streamlining, and (2) it is exploring with Gilpin County citizens ways and means to preserve the meaningful historical sites and to rebuild others in the Central City area.

"The opera group is trying to raise $200,000 to guarantee this season (one of the more exciting in recent years) and to assure future seasons. Coloradans really can't afford not to respond."

By March there was an appearance of hope along the horizon. President Neusteter told a press conference that the Association was "well on its way to recovery from the financial crisis." A budget of $528,000 for fiscal 1970-71 was proposed, but it would not cover opera. A financial campaign to be held at a later date would deal with this, the 1971 Festival, as well as retire existing debts, and support planning for further expansion, as well as the renovation of historical properties.

When the 1971 Festival was announced it listed Helen Hayes in Mary Chase's *Harvey*, Lillian Gish in an evening of reminiscences, and a series of ragtime piano programs with Max Morath, a Colorado Springs native. Finances permitting, opera would return. In *The Denver Post*, Pat Collins in her society column reassured readers the flower girls would again descend into the garden.

By strenuous efforts the Board cut the $190,000 deficit to $50,000.

Carl Dahlgren, the new executive director, pursued his concept of Central City as Williamsburg West, and invited Dr. Liston Leydendecker of Colorado State University to research the properties, with the hope he would find a new lode of tourist gold.

In April the 40th anniversary program was announced. There would be no opera. It opened at its peak with the endearing Lillian Gish recalling *Camille* at Central City as well as her moviemaking with D. W. Griffith.

Max Morath was pure fun, with a leavening of social commentary. Burgess Meredith had been due for his one-man show, *An Unpleasant Evening with H.L.Mencken*, but because of a disagreement between Meredith and its producer, it was canceled.

As replacement, Denver Lyric Theater's production of *The Medium* was brought from Denver for several performances, followed by music from the Colorado Philharmonic Orchestra of Evergreen, a performing ensemble constituted of outstanding instrumental students from across the nation.

Ill health forced Helen Hayes from *Harvey* to be replaced by an ailing Shirley Booth. Gig Young was the show in Mary Chase's play, the only play ever repeated at Central City, and he made an acute and winning Elwood P. Dowd who attracted good audiences through August. Miss Booth was not up to form, not measuring up to her memorable *The Time of the Cuckoo*.

Next came six days of *I Do, I Do*, with a lustreless Patrice Munsel and Stephen Douglass, a listless production made painful by the deterioration of Munsel's voice.

There were other additions, such as a folk dance festival but only at the start was this a very festive Festival.

Built to last in 1878, the Central City Opera House is encased in great rock walls which guard its wondrous interior defiantly. *Credit: Central City Opera House Association*

Many of those hickory chairs Peter McFarlane acquired in 1900 are embellished with the names of pioneers as well as great performers in the opera house. In 1987 the ceiling was given a splendid renovation. *Credit: Central City Opera House Association*

Anne Evans brought great integrity and imagination to the renovation and revitalization of opera in Central City.
*Credit: Colorado Historical Society*

Ida Kruse McFarlane married into the McFarlane family and thus the opera house was in her blood. With Anne Evans, she affirmed a dedication to theater of fine quality.
*Credit: Central City Opera House Association*

Robert Edmond Jones was ranked high among the forces in American theater when he came to Central City to produce, direct, and design *Camille* with Lillian Gish in 1932. *Credit: Colorado Historical Society*

Frank St. Leger first came to Central City in 1934 to conduct *Central City Nights*, and after the war produced some of the house's finest work. At his left is genial Frank Ricketson who led the Opera House Association from 1941 until 1964. *Credit: Colorado Historical Society*

Emerson Buckley came in 1956 to conduct *The Ballad of Baby Doe* and stayed 13 years, leading operas by Mozart, Rossini, Puccini, and Verdi, and the world premiere of Robert Ward's *The Lady from Colorado*.
*Credit: Central City Opera House Association*

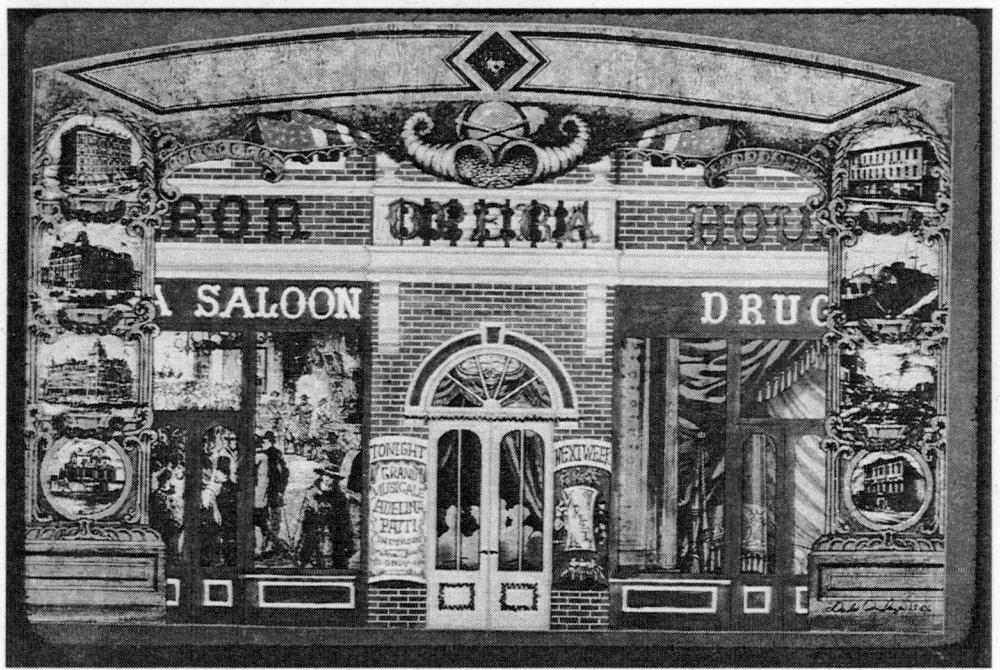

The colorful Leadville Street scene designed for Act I, Scene 1 of *The Ballad of Baby Doe* by Donald Oenslager. *Credit: Colorado Historical Society*

Oenslager's design for Act I, Scene 6 of the reception room at The Willard Hotel in Washington, D.C. where Baby Doe marries H.A.W. Tabor. *Credit: Colorado Historical Society*

Opening night curtain call of *The Ballad of Baby Doe* July 7, 1956. Left to right, composer Douglas Moore, conductor Emerson Buckley, Walter Cassel as Tabor, Martha Lipton as Augusta, Dolores Wilson as Baby Doe, libretto author John Latouche, co-director Hanya Holm, co-director Edwin Levy, designer Donald Oenslager, and Beatrice Krebs as Mama McCourt. *Credit: Colorado Historical Society*

With admirable artistry, Elemer Nagy directed and designed memorable productions of *Don Pasquale* and *The Merry Wives of Windsor*.
*Credit: Louise Pote.*

Nathaniel Merrill brought new theatrical dimensions to Central City with his stunning productions of *Aida, Lucia di Lammermoor, The Girl of the Golden West,* and *Don Giovanni.*
*Credit: Central City Opera House Association.*

Beverly Sills was Aida, and not as she had taken for granted, Lucia di Lammermoor. Never again was she Aida. *Credit: Louise Pote.*

Robert Darling brought a keen sense of innovation with him in 1978, enlivening the repertory and starting a composers-in-residence program.
*Credit: Central City Opera House Association*

John Moriarty came in 1978 to conduct *Don Pasquale*, and again in 1979 for *The Barber of Seville* and *The Medium*, and 1980 for *La Traviata*. In 1983 he returned as Artistic Director, and since then has led the Festival.
*Credit: Central City Opera House Association.*

# A NEW START

By the end of July almost all indebtedness had been retired, and Frances Melrose reported this matter of relief in the *Rocky Mountain News* with its accompanying evidence that the organization desired a return to opera.

Just in time for Thanksgiving it was announced the Nathaniel Merrill had committed himself to staging opera again in Central City through 1974. Because of the financial recovery this good news was possible.

Neusteter called for inclusion of contemporary opera in future plans, proposing a Forum for Contemporary Opera during which six unknown works would be studied and followed by concert performances in order, as Neusteter said, to "uncover suitable works for operatic presentation."

In *The Denver Post* Glenn Giffin pointed out that the lamentable example of *The Lady From Colorado* would not have taken place had its possible merits and problems been reviewed in some kind of a reading.

A "permanent opera company" was called for by Neusteter, one which would perform the year round, and would tour through Colorado and neighboring states. Neusteter, having delivered himself of his good notions, stepped down and out of office to be replaced by John Fleming Kelly.

Again it was confirmed that Merrill would become artistic director for 1972, with a 15-performance season to open July 1.

Though the 1971 Festival had varied in quality, box office receipts were $241,240.40, based on some 57 performances, including the play. A Neusteter fashion show brought in as much as $50,000, and over $10,000 came from Teller House tours.

Neusteter's support for contemporary opera had not vanished with his departure. In January 1971 Dahlgren announced a program for modern opera, with studio performances and at least one full production to be given during 1972. The plan called for bringing sixteen young singing talents to Central City to be coached and directed with composers in attendance. A three-day showcase of modern opera would then be offered, and a television taping would be made. A budget of $55,663 was set for this program.

In February there was heavy thinking about Central City and its preservation. National Park Service representatives came together with Central City board members and others to lay the groundwork of Colorado Citizens for Central City. There was talk of a master plan which could involve the Department of Urban Renewal, the Department of Housing, the Farmer's Home Administration, and even the Small Business Administration.

Some matters were more urgent than others. Negotiations with AGMA were up again, and contracts were not yet settled. Homer Reed chaired a fund-raising campaign for $200,000 in the course of which he underscored the fact that "the funds we are seeking serve to care for the operating deficit created by the limited seating capacity of the beautiful opera house."

In January Merrill was in Denver for talks with Dahlgren and the board, and announced that Robert O'Hearn, Merrill's designer of choice in the 60s at Central City and The Met, would again work with him there, and that Leonard Altman would be responsible for contemporary music and recitals.

By March, Merrill had decided the repertory would consist of Mozart's *The Marriage of Figaro* and Verdi's *Falstaff*. James Conlon, a brilliant 22-year old who had led *Boris Godunov* at Spoleto in 1971 would lead the Verdi in its Central City premiere, while Ernst Maerzendorfer of the Salzburg Mozarteum would conduct the Mozart.

Merrill planned to emphasize fresh, young talents at Central City, and announced that on August 13-15 four young composers would present their works. He knew there would be risks, but he had thought about them and was encouraged to take well-considered risks.

Very shortly after she won the 1972 Metropolitan Opera Auditions, Merrill signed Christine Weidinger along with an up-and-coming young mezzo Frederica von Stade to alternate as Cherubino. Santa Fe wanted Miss von Stade for Melisande in the Debussy opera, so she was released, and that was the performance which began her illustrious career.

Christine Weidinger was likewise a bright talent of the kind Merrill wished to feature. Runner-up to Miss Weidinger was Samuel Ramey, the former member of the Central City Opera chorus. Jan Redick, who had placed second, came to sing Barbarina. Thomas Halvorsen of Denver had also ranked high in these auditions, but was not invited to Central City.

Though special recognition of young singers was made, there was no lack of such familiar Central City figures as Frank Guarrera in his seventh season to sing Falstaff in its five performances. Because of this short schedule there would be no doubling of *Falstaff* roles. Catherine Malfitano, Leo Goeke, Carol Bayard, Russell Christopher, and Carolyne James made a strong Verdi cast.

Donal Henehan of *The New York Times* reviewed with almost no reservations regarding *Falstaff*, a production he believed would "make one listener doubt he would ever enjoy one more anywhere," referring to its "boisterously rakish and inventive production," with the benefit of musical leadership by James Conlon "who conducted one of the most demanding ensemble scores in opera with immense polish and incisiveness."

I found "the central glory is Falstaff himself, the beautifully fulfilled creation by Frank Guarrera of Sir John, the living blimp, the great appetite, the complete sensual male - run to seed! The facial animation Guarrera brings, the delicate walk, the gusto and the dismay, all that leads Sir John forward. Guarrera's vocal characterization is ripe, and nothing of this technique did other than strengthen the vitality of the performance."

Guarrera had sung Ford for Toscanini in the famed broadcast which had stimulated a renewed interest in the opera, and a recording of the performance was released in 1954, so he had been intensely involved with the opera for many years.

The *Figaro* offered Paul Plishka as Figaro, Robert Goodloe as the Count, Patricia Brooks as the Countess, and Benita Valente as Susanna, with Christine Weidinger as Cherubino in the first cast.

Lenus Carlson was the imposing alternate Count, with Kathryn Bouleyn the Countess, Margery Ryan the Susanna, and Barbara Martin the Cherubino, and John Seabury the Figaro.

To me the production was "incomparably delightful entertainment... When Mozart's music, the Beaumarchais comedy, Nathaniel Merrill's superb theatrical taste, and Robert O'Hearn's feeling for color and design come together wonders happen."

Henehan found the orchestra under Maerzendorfer to be weak when it did not offend him, but he thought the cast "respectable right down the line, (with) Benita Valente as a witty, pure-voiced Susanna" and Patricia Brooks as the Countess, though he acknowledged Brooks got off to a shaky beginning after which she improved. He thought Plishka's Figaro and Goodloe's Count were overly stentorian, with a tendency to overwhelm the women vocally, and that Plishka "boomed and bellowed far too much."

Shirley Fleming of *Musical America* admired "three splendid portrayals: Paul Plishka's Figaro, virile affable, vigorous, and nobody's buffoon; Benita Valente's Susanna; and Robert Goodloe's Count, debonair, arrogant, and thoroughly attractive," though she found soprano Brooks "off-stride in her opening aria, with a dry and reedy tone, but (she) got back into familiar good form by the arrival of 'Dove sono' and was unfailingly warm as a personality."

Henehan thought much was to be done "before Central City can stand up as a major festival. Creeping honky-tonkyism is taking over Eureka Street, but the tourists may still see a few valid phenomena in town, such as the Glory Hole, an abandoned mine, The Face on the Bar Room Floor at the Teller House, or the square dancers at Williams Stable."

"Mr. Merrill and Mr. Dahlgren, the festival's executive director," he went on to say, "know they will not be able to pull this improbable town to the level of Salzburg or Glyndebourne overnight if indeed that is their joint intention. But with *Falstaff* at least, Central City has shown that such a thing might be done, and perhaps before 1976, too."

Shortly after the Festival got under way I talked with Merrill who told me "There was barely time to pick up the reins where they were," in reference to the 1972 season. At that time he was thinking of a revival of his distinguished 1963 production of *Don*

*Giovanni,* and even more stimulating was the idea of doing both Shakespeare and Verdi *Othellos* on alternate evenings.

"Widening the base of support" was the biggest project ahead, and it seemed that the double triumphs of the 1972 season would go far to assure such a positive development. He felt O'Hearn's strong and elegant settings for the two productions had much to do with their success. He told me O'Hearn had achieved the feeling of spaciousness on the small stage by designing for a thirty-five foot stage width, even though the proscenium was but twenty-five feet wide, and otherwise made use of forced perspectives.

The diversity this summer was dazzling. Leonard Altman was busy organizing a schedule of special events including chamber music and piano recitals. William Warfield as Gianni Schicchi with apprentice performers, a Vaughan Williams church service, Poulenc's *La Voix Humaine,* the Art Pepper Jazz Combo were but some of the musical offerings. On stage there would be touring productions of *Private Lives* with Marsha Mason, directed by Francis Ford Coppola of *The Godfather, 1776,* and George Gobel in *The Last of the Red Hot Lovers.*

Merrill had been quoted by Henehan as aiming at making the Central City company "the best musical ensemble in the world," and for this he required a budget of $160,000. The National Endowment for the Arts had made a grant of $40,000, which brought a welcome turn of financial security, but it was not a large amount.

Finances were carefully controlled. There was an indebtedness of $96,000, of which $63,000 was accumulated prior to 1972, and $33,000 was from 1972 despite the raising of $256,000. Total revenue for this active season was $543,000, with expenses of $576,000.

Having had an operatic sell-out with the largest ticket sales in history, the Association recognized that a force larger than itself was threatening control of the Central City Opera Festival. There had been rumors of Board concern over Leonard Altman, and it seemed he was being used as a whipping boy. The real target was Merrill whose command of operatic effort was Napoleonic in the view of the Board. The Board wished to believe it had some piece of the reins. Merrill had shown the energy and intelligence behind his vision. The deficit of his season was smaller than it had been in twenty years.

The combination of the far-sighted ambitions of Dahlgren and the imaginative Merrill was more than the Board could face. In October a press release announced that Robert F. Lotito, a former Board member and long time Denver film publicity man, had been named Executive Director following "the expiration of a contract with the Dahlgren Arts Management, Inc."

Merrill's three-year contract was not canceled, although Kelly announced that he had been "invited but chose not to return" to Central City as Artistic Director for the 1973 Festival. Although in his speech President Kelly seemed to accept the ongoing Twentieth Century Program, it was later confirmed it would not be receiving a comparable emphasis.

In a letter made public, Merrill wrote to the Board that "My participation in this year's Festival was a most gratifying experience, and I'm proud to have helped restore opera to Central City. It is therefore with a profound sense of loss that I write this in the realization that my ideals involving the establishment of the Festival as an artistic venture of national and international importance cannot be realized by me under the conditions set forth."

These conditions were chiefly that Altman not return, as he had stepped on too many sets of toes, and was thought to be arrogant and unappreciative of Board efforts. Merrill felt the limitations set up by the executive committee over the hiring of his artistic staff were excessive.

President Kelly expressed a belief the Association should concentrate on opera and theater production, and some one else should restore and maintain the historically important Central City properties, which numbered around forty. Dahlgren had worked to integrate these properties with the Festival, and thus expand the historical references of the town, but this policy now was overturned.

At the same meeting at which Lotito was named Executive Director the Board was asked to consider a Resolution of Policies and Objectives for the Association, recommended by the Executive Committee, and presented to the Board by Kelly.

It called first for a working relationship of the Central City Opera House Association with the Denver Lyric Opera "into a strong unified body with a large dedicated membership and a professional staff capable of producing opera of excellent quality," with productions sufficiently professional to be done in the proposed Denver Center for the Performing Arts, and on tour. This year-round professional organization, it was resolved, would be well-equipped in connection with the Denver Center for the Performing Arts to mount the annual summer Central City Festival."

A final provision called for "work with the University of Denver and donors of the Association's Central City properties or a separation of the responsibilities related to the preservation and restoration of Central City from those related to the presentation of the Festival."

In January it was announced that Edwin MacArthur was to become artistic administrator for 1973. MacArthur was musical director of the Eastman Opera Theater, former director of the St. Louis Municipal Opera, and a long-time protegee and accompanist of soprano Kirsten Flagstad. He would be assisted by David Effron, Artistic Administrator and Assistant to director Max Rudolph at the Curtis Institute at Philadelphia, who would conduct one of the two operas that would be done in the reduced schedule of fifteen performances.

In February it was announced that *Falstaff* would be given a revival of five performances, its sell-out in the previous year seeming to promise continuing interest. Also, *The Barber of Seville*, that tireless comedy, would be done again after eight years. David Effron would conduct the Verdi, and Maerzendorfer would come for the Rossini, with Ralph Herbert coming to stage the productions.

A budget of $502,000 was proposed, of which $242,000 was for year-round expenses, in which maintenance of the properties and staff salaries were the principal elements. Festival expenses would be $260,000. A campaign to raise $300,000 was planned. The 1972 campaign had succeeded in raising $256,361.

To Glenn Giffin of *The Denver Post* it seemed the operas were "staid" and that a "step backward had been taken" with specific regard to the elimination of "special concerts and workshop performances that had given Central City something of a Spoleto West flavor, of something happening in every courtyard and street corner."

He went on to suggest that MacArthur had a misunderstanding of what 1973 was all about in saying he would not do "esoteric performances," referring to the essentials of that program, the hearing of young professionals as well as of new music. Giffin concluded that " At best, 1973 promises to be a stopgap; at worse, the first step of a lingering decline."

In April, President Kelly stressed the hope of the organization for qualifying for national foundation support although earlier it had been said that such foundations were disinterested in opera companies because they were limited to single seasons; the idea of getting Central City together with Denver Lyric Opera was largely because of such possible problems.

Donald Seawell of the Denver Center for the Performing Arts arranged an August visit by *The Hollow Crown* with its imposing cast of Sir Michael Redgrave, Dame Peggy Ashcroft, Roy Dotrice, and Brewster Mason. John Barton who devised this historical entertainment for the Royal Shakespeare Company would direct.

The season opened with *The Barber of Seville* led by Joseph Blatt, since Maerzendorfer was ill in Salzburg and unable to travel. Dominic Cossa was an ebullient Figaro but director Ralph Herbert favored physical comedy, and everything was very broadly laughable.

In Robert O'Hearn's delectable sets Judith Dickson was a fresh-voiced, attractive Rosina with David Sundquist an affable, Almaviva of considerable vocal polish. Malcolm Smith relished the low comedy of Don Basilio and his snuff-box routine. Frederick Burchinal, a recent graduate of the Lamont School of Music, showed his potential in the small roles of Fiorello and the Sergeant.

It was good to have *Falstaff* back even if director Herbert could not begin to match the fine timing and movement of Merrill's 1972 production. For Frank Guerrera, Carol Bayard, and Russell Christopher there was the opportunity of improving upon their original performances. The new cast members were barely adequate and gave emphasis to the money-minded concerns of the Board.

After the operas came a week of *The Gershwin Years* with Barbara Cook, Nancy Dussault, Helen Gallagher, and Harold Lang, an aggregation which should have brought vibrant entertainment to such gracious material but the drab production and its made-for-TV style was a great disappointment.

This gave way to a week's run of an English comedy, *The Irregular Verb To Love* by Hugh and Margaret Williams, with Celeste Holm and Wesley Addy, and a young actor named Christopher Reeve.

This was followed by a gala benefit for the young artists which featured Dominic Cossa. Later, Eugenia Rawls, wife of Donald Seawell, gave two performances of her one-woman show on Tallullah Bankhead.

*The Hollow Crown* was an engaging effort despite its not being a true drama. Sir Michael was in poor health and in low energy but Dame Peggy Ashcroft was sublime and Roy Dotrice a complete delight.

In November the annual meeting received the doubly provocative announcement that starting in 1975 Central City would present opera in Denver, and that to support this opera and that at Central City a $1.5 million fund drive would be carried out. In 1974 a drive for $300,000 would be held, with annual increases scheduled.

President Kelly reported that indebtedness had been reduced by $33,000, though the sudden gasoline shortage was thought to have cost the Association and the town about $50,000, and a power outage during one matinee cost $5,000 in refunds. Talk of expanding public transportation to Central City for the duration of the fuel crisis was heard, as well as discussion of a temporary move to Denver until the crisis blew over.

The recurrent interest in doing new opera was again fueled, this time by two pledges of $5,000 each towards the cost of commissioning a new opera. Already, late in the summer of 1973, the 1976 Colorado Centennial Commission had made an award of $9,000 to the towns of Central City and Black Hawk for restoration for 1976.

The 1974 season was announced in January, and it made a bold inclusion of Benjamin Britten's *A Midsummer Night's Dream* and *Rigoletto*, for the first time since 1957. The Verdi would have twelve performances and the Britten would be given seven times. $180,000 was budgeted for the operas. The continuing gas shortage brought up consideration of alternative plans, and these led either to Loretto Heights College or to Colorado Women's College.

At the time it was thought the most interesting idea was to give emphasis to operas from Shakespearean sources, and such operas as *Romeo and Juliet*, *Macbeth*, and *Otello* were proposed for 1975 and 1976. There was further talk of a new opera that might be premiered in 1976.

The 1974 Festival began with a sidewalk art show on June 22 and concluded with a walking tour of the area on September 2, coinciding with the final day of an exhibit by the Rocky Mountain Weaver's Guild. In between there was a Count Basie concert, such one-act operas as Puccini's *Suor Angelica* and Hindemith's *There and Back*. A touring stage version of *Gigi* played two weeks to uniformly poor reviews, and lost money.

Bodo Igesz came from the Met for both operas. He had been Goeran Gentele's directorial assistant on the *Carmen* that was to inaugurate his position at the Met as General Manager and director. When Gentele and his wife were killed in an accident in Sicily, Igesz took over the reins of the production.

At his suggestion, Neil Peter Jampolis, who had designed ten productions for Igesz at the Santa Fe opera, was hired to design *Rigoletto*, and the fine old Central City hand, Robert O'Hearn signed on to do the Britten.

There was strong critical support for the carefully prepared *Dream* which Effron led with clarity and insight. Igesz proved a capable director who balanced the diverse action of the comedy.

O"Hearn's budget conscious settings were the only truly disappointing ones he ever did for Central City but there were moments of brilliance in the lighting which lit up faces as large, grotesque plants were moved about for different parts of the Athenian woods. There was just too much dark. The music accomplished the magic and the mystery.

There was novelty in having Frank Guarrera, a Falstaff, Scarpia, Rigoletto, and Tabor in past years, take on the role of Bottom, and he did it with total relish. Among the rustics who drew attention were James Hoback as Flute, and thus the Thisbe, and Richard Haile who was a jolly Quince.

Among the two couples, both David Sundquist and Thomas Jamerson appealed with the firm grace of their singing, while there was excessive vocal weight to Margaret Yauger's work and Mary Ellen Pracht was not up to her previous standards.

Christine Weidinger was a lustrous Tytania, vocally sure and bewitchingly beautiful, while John Ferrante's Oberon was admirably dark-hued and fascinating.

As for *Rigoletto*, it should have been renamed Gilda. In this role Benita Valente gave refinement and expression to a production that otherwise was weak in too many casting elements. Chester Ludgin's strongly conceived but vocally various approach to the title role gave it an uncertain center. Robert Moulson was dry of voice and charmless as the Duke. Shirley Love was a marvelously voluptuous Maddalena and Malcolm Smith a perversely dark Sparafucile. Stephen West in his first role at Central City was an imposing Monterone.

In the second cast, Adib Fazah, though light of voice, made a strong impression, minimizing the grotesque aspects of Rigoletto, and giving excellent musical line. Christine Weidinger scored again as Gilda, singing with an unmarred, beautiful line, and was genuinely affecting. Erik Townsend was a disaster as the Duke, lacking both voice and presence. As Maddalena, Margaret Yauger was animated but lustreless.

The Jampolis settings were sparse, poorly painted, and the effort to impose a contemporary style went amiss.

Glenn Giffin wrote of the production that "as far as directing goes, *Rigoletto* disappoints. The show needs a choreographer to make the opening act as bubbly as the music suggests. Couples pacing three steps and changing elbows don't really suggest a frivolous dance.

"But director Bodo Igesz lets other inanities go, too. Static tableaus haven't been an operatic tradition for the past twenty years, yet here they are."

Giffin did believe that in offering the Britten work, the Central City Opera had offered "a production of imagination and style, handsomely done up and sweeping the audience along with the enthusiasm of a three-ring circus." Anne Culver in the News called it a "significant step in the CCOHA's growth."

Depite the presence in its cast of Lois Hunt, Marcellina in the 1947 *Fidelio* and a lovely Perichole, and Earl Wrightson, who had once been noted for sparkle, *Gigi* lost over $30,000 in its two-week run, provoking CCOHA president Thomas Jefferson Herbert to observe that "unless we can at least budget a break-even, I don't see much chance of continuing theater."

Herbert pointed out that every time the opera house is used for opera there is a $7,000 loss, but often in the past this had been made up for by the play. But not in 1974. He believed the opera season had been enormously successful, though a deficit of $100,000 had been anticipated. This debt turned out to be slightly less, amounting to $80,985. The *Dream* had been a critical but not a financial success, and word of mouth did not spread on *Rigoletto*. Or else it did. The two productions cost $572,882.

Following this season, four matters required attention. One, the cost of producing the Festival, particularly the operas, was greater than the income potential. Secondly, past deficits were not put to rest, and thirdly, new deficits would be added, and thus, fourthly, a source of capital was needed.

The aged properties would not cease requiring attention. New sewer connections were costing $12,000.

Some courageous thinking went into setting up the 1975 season, even if it turned out that there were insufficient casting resources to do justice both to Cavalli's *Scipio Africanus* and Mozart's *Don Giovanni*. The Cavalli, composed in 1664, would be an American premiere, and represented a new kind of repertory for Central City. In 1974 Cavalli's *L'Egisto* was done with success at Santa Fe, so there were interesting elements of competition in this offering.

Because *Gigi* had been such a bomb no play was scheduled. William Windom did a single performance of his Thurber show. The Apprentice Artists did Wolf-Ferrari's *The Four Ruffians*, prepared by Felix Popper, showing the talents of James Hoback, Glenn Martin, and Cornel Richie.

Bodo Igesz, author of the English version of *Scipio*, returned to direct both Cavalli and Mozart. Robert O'Hearn was back in engaging form for the Cavalli but the Mozart was designed by his student, Gary Chalmers.

For *Scipio*, O'Hearn devised all kinds of theatrical wonders - a descending cloud bearing the Goddess of Love, a flying bird, and the Carthaginian navy rocking at berth as waves rolled onto the shore, and those with a taste for musical antiquities found it much to their taste.

Igesz cast the Cavalli with care, framing the lovely Veronica Tyler in this charming production, and bringing in such practiced vocal stylists as Charles Bressler and John Ferrante, along with such charming new talents as Betsy Norden, Thomas Jamerson, James Hoback, and Michael Myers.

Audiences arrived in a state of curiosity only to be pleasantly surprised by the degree of pleasure attained. Glenn Giffin thought it was an "absolute romp," and Anne Culver called it a "masterful production." It was a treat to look at, with O'Hearn's unfussy but opulent settings, and Suzanne Mess's elegant costuming.

Veronica Tyler suffused the entire performance with her personal dark beauty and memorably fine singing. Conductor David Effron led a particularly good playing of the orchestral score.

*Don Giovanni* did not come off well, partially because of an uninteresting set, largely because of the dark in which just about everything transpired, and mostly because of excessive emoting by the cast, with more clutching and grabbing of arms than the requisite style could bear.

Casting was uneven with a brusque Don from Malcolm Smith, a beguiling Zerlina from Betsy Norden and a beauteous Elvira from Christine Weidinger though there was an element of strain in her singing. Noelle Rogers was in moments a spectacular alternate Donna Anna but quality was not sustained.

A crude *Don Giovanni* was unneeded.

The numbers were not good for this season, and deficits mounted. Bob Baker, now president, worked on reducing the deficit and getting better economic functioning. He envisaged three groups, the summer Festival, historic preservation, and production and presentation of opera in Denver.

In April it had been announced that the Seattle Opera, widely hailed as an outstanding new regional company, would bring *Aida* to Denver with "an Outstanding Cast of Nationally Known Singers."

It seemed that Seattle had committed itself to bring a first-rate production, one to be supervised by its general director, Glynn Ross, directed by its chief director, Lincoln Clark, and conducted by Henry Holt, its principal conductor.

The singers had never been together in an *Aida*, so it was not a proper touring company but one that opened and closed in Denver. The inadequate singers were Rolf Bjoerling, son of the great Jussi, as Rhadames, Betty Jones as Aida, Marguerite Yauger as Amneris, with only Robert Mosley's Amonasro, Archie Drake's Ramfis, and Stephen West's King the exceptions to poor casting. West, a Denver, native, was the one singer who could be readily understood.

Duain Wolfe gave attention to a strong, local chorus, while Mattlyn Gavers and Maria Ferra pulled off a kind of miracle in finding good dancers for the triumphal entry scene. Henry Holt's leadership of the Denver Symphony Orchestra was pedestrian, and its musicians were irked by his condescending attitude. Insufficient attention to the poor acoustics of the Auditorium Theater, stemming largely from the pit's shallowness, was one major problem. The ornate, Italian-made settings were cheap looking and there was no dramatic resonance in the performance.

This was a setback to the Association as a strong sales pitch had sold out the two performances. The Association had to contend with the major disappointment. So large-scaled a disaster killed a relationship with Seattle which the Association had hoped would lead to further collaboration. With a loud thud, touring opera ended.

President Baker announced the possibility of presenting in Central City a new musical, *Western Star*, by Dale Wasserman, author of *Man of La Mancha*. Lotito described the work as a "cornball Western, with the same appeal as *Oklahoma*." That was the last heard of this project.

That $100,000 indebtedness loomed over the Association, and Baker hoped to get rid of it by 1976, as well as gathering $355,000 to finance the Festival. He also hoped that by 1978 attendance could be raised to 90% of capacity.

Performing in Denver was not put down by the *Aida* flop but it continued to be stimulated by the Denver Center for the Performing Arts, financed by the Bonfils Foundation; its funding came from profits of *The Denver Post* and after its purchase by the Times-Mirror Corporation, owners of *The Los Angeles Times*, from the profits of that sale.

The Association had the idea that it could become a "wing" of the DCPA. There was concern that planned alterations of the Auditorium Theater to a 1700-seat house from its 2200 seat capacity would bring financial problems by limiting profits from seat sales. Nothing ever came of this.

For a big anniversary, the 100th anniversary of the building of the opera house, many had expected a large-scale celebration. Another revival of *The Ballad of Baby Doe* did not quite satisfy. Emerson Buckley, the original conductor, returned for a lively but unexceptional production, featuring Frederick Burchinal as a vigorous Tabor with Adib Fazah, his light-voiced alternate.

Neither of the Baby Does realized the fragile, beautiful character. Gianni Rolandi was exuberant but insensitive while Paula Seibel lacked focus in her weak performance. Both Augustas missed her strength and vulnerability.

The best news was that the opera showed its eternal popularity, and the numbers at the box-office were very good.

The urge to do opera in Denver was fulfilled on a high level in November when *La Boheme* was impressively mounted in the Auditorium Theater for two performances.

That Central City could mount superior productions had long been proven, and here it was in Denver with that special individuality and care. Bodo Igesz was the stage director and David Effron conducted, with Duain Wolfe as chorus master, and sets by John Wright Stevens.

Benita Valente was a Mimi of great artistry, while George Shirley was throughout sensitive and meaningful, though tight at the top of his tenor. Ryan Edwards was a skillful Marcello while Ashley Putnam bloomed stunningly as Musetta. She had had a very real success in 1976 at Santa Fe in Virgil Thomson's *The Mother of Us All*, and here was another success. Opera of quality could be done in Denver or wherever there was the imagination and patience to take pains.

1976 was a very good year, Baker told the Association in January at its annual meeting. An unofficial figure of $27,498 was given as the profit for 1976. There was a continuing deficit of $100,000, refinanced by the United Bank of Denver as debt consolidation. A $200,000 limit was set on production costs for 1977. A budget of $100,000 was set for Denver productions.

Baker could indeed take pride in the raising of $317,766 in 1976, the most ever raised for the Association in a single campaign. Income derived was $228,713 for the annual campaign, plus $28,953 for opera in Denver. These figures comprised 49% of the income. Box office revenues were $167,188 at Central City, and $52,651 for *La Boheme* in Denver. Property rentals, parking fees, and miscellaneous items put $72,611 into the pot, while other special activities, such as fashion shows, brought in $31,515.

The productions cost $368,187, and staff and general expenses were $173,119.

In comparison with other regional companies, the 49% which Central City raised exceeded funds raised by other cities for opera. The 92% capacity attained in 1976 was admirable, and even more so was the nearly 100% capacity for the Denver *La Boheme* in the 2200-seat Auditorium Theater.

At one point a Mozart festival was contemplated for 1977. The ideal combination of *The Magic Flute* and *Cosi Fan Tutte* was urged, for such a billing would have redeemed the Association's too frequent forgetfulness as far as Mozart operas were concerned. *Cosi* had not been done since 1948, and *The Magic Flute,* so ideal for this theater, had not ever been done.

The nod, however, was given to two repeats; one, *A Midsummer Night's Dream*, was recent enough to be a repeat, while *The Bartered Bride* was the first opera to be done after the reopening of the opera house. Its 1940 performance was long cherished as a high-water mark in the first decade of the revival years. The Britten would have six performances, the Smetana 14.

The Smetana comedy was done on a setting by Jack Barkla that was borrowed from the Minnesota Opera Company, so steeply raked one feared a cart brought on stage would plunge into the orchestra pit.

Though the production did not originate with Central City, as tradition had established productions there should do. it was in all aspects charming, delivering the music in attentive, thriving manner, touched by imagination, as in a pantomime during the overture which set the background for the story.

Winsome Glenys Fowles convinced as Marenka in the first cast, with Henry Price, handsome of manner and voice, as Jenik. Philip Steele ingratiated as the marriage broker, and Michael Crouse was the Vasek, a role happily not overdone in this production.

In the alternate cast, Beverly Flower gave what Glenn Giffin called a "gilded and gifted performance," but he found tenor George Livings slow to reach "the peak of his voice," and found his acting wanting. Michael Myers as Vasek he found sympathetic and effective.

The Britten repeat had good ensemble and the production worked well though with fewer outstanding voices than in 1974. Gwendolyn Bradley, now at the Met and highly regarded elsewhere, was a wonderful Tytania but John Ferrante's counter-tenor showed wear and tear not evident in the earlier production.

David Sundquist was an outstanding Lysander, and former apprentice Stephen West stirred attention with his notable, noble Duke. In the acting role of Puck, Dana Bashor, a University of Denver student, performed with relish.

In September, Robert E. Darling was named artistic director of the Central City Opera House Association, Taking on what President Baker described as the role of "principal professional artistic advisor." Darling was "principally a designer and stage director," as Baker noted, "and his responsibilities would include those functions for some of our productions. But he and the Association agreed that within budget limitations he will engage other directors and designers for some of our productions. We all feel that this is artistically sound for the Association."

# THE DARLING YEARS

Darling had been active as a designer for the San Francisco Opera, including *The Visit of the Old Lady*, Von Einem's operatic version of Friedrich Durenmatt's play. For the Santa Fe Opera he had designed its *Don Carlo*, and for the Kansas City Opera in 1973 he both staged and designed *The Flying Dutchman*, which was also seen in Louisville and Hartford. He restyled Wieland Wagner's *Salome* production for the San Francisco Opera, where he also recreated Wolfram Skalicki's design for *Parsifal*, adding a slowly revolving, lopsided disc, a successful innovation.

In 1972 for the San Francisco spring season he designed, with William Francisco directing, the Brech-Weill *Mahagonny* in a production San Francisco critic Arthur Bloomfield described as "a magnificently salty, batty production, deadpan, but compassionate, for which director Francisco and designer Darling can take much credit."

Darling grew up in Oakland, in the shade of San Francisco's high-arching importance, and attended San Francisco State College. His first job was as a design assistant at the New York City Opera. Ann Farris, his wife, was Executive Director of Opera America, in Washington, D.C.

Within the month, Darling brought forth the Central City Company Singers, an ensemble partly supported by the Colorado Council on the Arts and Humanities in a concert sponsored by the United Bank of Denver. Two operas, including Samuel Barber's *A Hand of Bridge*, were done, along with some Barber songs and the Brahms *Liebeslieder Waltzes*, all under the direction of Duain Wolfe, chorus master since 1975 for the Central City Festival.

Darling lost no time in talking of the Central City Opera House Association's future, telling Glenn Giffin he had a "fascination with the hall, and I've been impressed with the quality of production and acoustics. I'm concerned with making a Festival that is the whole city and not just the opera house. There should be an effort to involve townspeople and get the Festival into the 'other' street of Central City. The segregation is glaring," going on to observe that "the nature of the Festival has its ups and downs."

"The mantle of responsibility that Central City carries with it is something I've been very aware of as something it achieved in the 30s with Robert Edmond Jones."

Talking about opera in Denver, Darling said it was "important to do opera in a traditional way and lead audiences," and of local opera activity, "I think that all of the opera activity, as in New York, even if the quality is terrible, gives singers an opportunity to perform. But there are dangers. It can use singers' voices beyond their capacity and encourage 'traditions' that are grotesque. On the purely abstract level, any group that is working towards opera theater I welcome."

Three goals for Central City were spoken of. Expansion of repertory, encouragement of audiences, and creation of an "American singer-actor, capable of moving, developing a character, and being musically sound." Darling spoke for himself and for a growing number of opera-lovers when he said "I like to hear opera in the original language, but I also feel opera is a form of communication, and when neither the audience nor singers understand the language this makes total mockery of the form. It is a very difficult problem, and one which has become snobbish in its acceptance. I would rather have young artists make the dramatic connection."

Finances were in ominous shape when the annual meeting was held in January, and Edward E. Bolle, the new president, although not previously a board member, told the Association that there was indebtedness of $260,754. Carrick Hill had been in line for the presidency and very active, but as president of The Denver department stores he had been transferred to New York City. Bolle was his replacement. Hill would return later for another involvement.

Attendance had been down to 62% capacity in 1977, and though both productions had good reviews, there were not the names, the glitter, the productions to draw strongly.

Thomas Jefferson Herbert was a paid executive as Director of Finance, but this arrangement did not last. By the time *Salome* was presented in March of 1981 during opening week at the Boettcher Concert Hall in Denver, Herbert was gone from the board, and Dennis Baldwin now chaired the finance and budget committee.

In January Bolle had said there would be a 1978 season "if at all possible."

On March 4, 1978, the 100th anniversary of the opening of the opera house in Central City, there was a celebration with Joe Wheeler of Central City telling the history, and there were selections from *The Bohemian Girl* and from Gilbert and Sullivan, and cake and carnations for all. About 125 attended this "re-dedication."

In mid-March, president Bolle scheduled a Board Orientation Program at the Denver Country Club, and for the first time in too many years an effort was made to communicate with the Denver musical community in the belief that its support was crucial to resolution of the Central City financial plight.

Darling took a look at the in-the-round Boettcher Concert Hall, and reported that "when I look at the hall I see a manipulation of tensions in space. *Salome* fits perfectly into this space because the opera embodies a pull of two forces which control all the action: the moon which symbolizes the outer world, and John The Baptist who represents the inner vision."

So, *Salome* it was, and just a bit more problematical than usual because of this uncertainty of focus. Added to this, the problems of doing opera in the round were very real and Darling had not had experience with doing opera in such a venue. There was also too little time to consider this problem in all aspects.

To compound difficulties, two weeks before the *Salome* performances, Robert Lotito resigned the executive managership of the Association although he would stay on through May 1. In a statement to the press, Lotito said his long association with the Central City Opera was "interesting and frustrating as well as rewarding."

Darling's *Salome* design was adventuresome. Without proscenium, he used guy ropes from the depths of the cistern to the ceiling, holding the corners of the playing area in a huge swing. Other ropes built angular designs into the scene, all this stressing the height of the area. Strong theater lighting was not available and this was a loss, but costuming was brilliantly conceived.

"Handsome use," I wrote, "was made of the stage trapdoors for the cistern in which Jokanaan is held. His ascent to the terrace was on a rope sling, making strong physical drama. I missed having a moon, as much for the dramatic focus it would have provided as for the importance to the drama of there being a visible moon. Striking as it was, the descent from his tower by the Executioner went against the growling depths attained here by the music .... It was however a visually stunning moment."

A key flaw was that the singing in English was nearly incomprehensible. The major weakness was that Louise Pearl, the Salome, was a cipher, so palid a presence that the production was close to being a *Salome* without a Salome. She was indistinct and though there was some lustre in the voice there was no wantonness, no intensity, no insinuation.

When the Jokaanen, William Chapman, became indisposed, Chester Ludgin substituted, delivering an excellent portrayal. He could be heard and understood, and his vocal strength gave needed intensity to the character.

Alan Crofoot's Herod looked like Charles Laughton's Nero, expanded to enormous proportions. His singing was impressive. His operatic opportunities were limited by his size, and this apparently was a factor in his subsequent tragic suicide.

Among several local singers who were heard to good advantage were Lynn Wickenden as the Page, Herbert Eckhoff as the First Nazarene, David Hall as the Second Nazarene, and Scot Weir as one of the Jews.

The score was conducted with commanding comprehension by Stefan Minde and performed by Denver Symphony players in their pit beneath the stage.

*Salome* was well chosen to introduce opera at Boettcher Concert Hall. The problematical acoustics interfered little with voices which projected well and enunciated carefully, but the others were lost. It would be five years before opera would again be fully staged in Boettcher Concert Hall. The Central City Opera House Association has never since staged opera in Denver. The problems of Denver theaters suitable for opera remain unresolved to this day.

Late in April president Bolle sent out a Monday Memo which chortled mildly at the fact that no more than $6,000 was lost in doing *Salome*.

In May, Bolle announced the appointment of Peter N. Kellogg as Managing Director of the Association. Kellogg came from Boston where had had served with ARTS/Boston, Inc. which served the city through collective marketing and public information programs on the arts. Earlier he had chaired the Allocations Committee of the Connecticut Commission on the Arts, and before this he worked ten years for Connecticut General Life Insurance.

Kellogg hardly had come aboard when in June the Association received a "dramatic challenge." Suddenly it had been realized that on June 14, one day before the start of New York rehearsals for the 1978 season, a check for $70,000 was due to cover salaries. An appeal to the Board resulted in a quick gathering of $35,000, while a review of previous commitments indicated there were enough funds to guarantee $100,000 in short term bank loans. There was enough money to go ahead with the 1978 Festival.

With the pledging of $70,000, the goal of $350,000 could be dropped back to $280,000.

The 1978 operas were to include Balfe's *The Bohemian Girl* and Donizetti's invariably popular *Don Pasquale*. It was the Balfe work which in 1874 at Central City's Belvidere Theater had raised funds for the building of the new opera house, to replace the one destroyed by fire, as well as to assist the town's recovery from a major disaster.

There would be eleven performances of *The Bohemian Girl* and six of the Donizetti comedy.

Darling was determined to have strength in staff, and not do all the directing and designing himself. He directed and designed the Balfe while William Francisco, with whom he had worked at the San Francisco Opera on *Mahoganny*, came to direct *Don Pasquale*, which was designed by Miguel Romero.

John Moriarty, formerly of the New England Conservatory of Music, now of the Opera Department of Boston Conservatory of Music, and at the Santa Fe Opera, a conductor, stage director, and director of apprentice programs, came to conduct the Donizetti and to lead the apprentice programs. Paul Polivnick, associate conductor of the Indianapolis Symphony, came for the Balfe.

With its dated melodramatics done without camp, and with emphasis on Balfe's tuneful songs, *The Bohemian Girl* was one to relish. There was charm in the naivite of the orchestral interludes. Many rousing choruses, including a miniature madrigal, all spirited and in their day highly popular were given sparkle by the Central City Chorus, prepared by Duain Wolfe.

Leigh Munroe as the heroine, Arline, enchanted with her beauty and rich soprano, and her presence. Vinson Cole as Thadeus had been a Metropolitan Auditions winner in 1977, and had been noted in a small role in Falla's *La Vida Breve* at Santa Fe in 1975. He has since gone on to the New York City Opera and from there to the Metropolitan Opera. His voice seemed to have a rare richness. His acting had a distance to go.

As Devilshoof, Peter Strummer, Bottom in the 1977 revival of Britten's *Dream*, continued to demonstrate a distinctive acting style and fine singing.

From the hilarious, rained-out picnic pantomimed during the overture, to the trumpet serenade which accompanied Ernesto's shaving, *Don Pasquale* was filled with the surprises of Francisco's quick-witted stage direction. It produced the amplitude of laughter this wonderful opera should bring.

Susan Smith was beauteous and vocally vivacious as Norina but Spiro Malas continued to lack the basic instincts for Pasquale; David Hall's Ernesto had flair, while Dominic Cossa was an assured, ingratiating Malatesta. Moriarty made dazzling fun of this music, while the opera was fine to look at with Miguel Romero's deft settings and Suzanne Mess's pleasing costumes.

During the summer there was a premiere in the Teller House bar, when *The Face on the Barroom Floor* was introduced. It was commissioned by the CCOHA from Henry Mollicone, with a book by John S. Bowman, adapted from the doggerel by H. Antoine D'Arcy which related to the Herndon Davis painting, done in 1936, which attracts people to this bar to see The Face that is on the floor.

This opera was about twenty minutes long, and flashed back from the present day to mining times for a tragic incident, then returned to the present for a re-play of the same violent denouement.

During his 1979 visit to Central City Andrew Porter from *The New Yorker* saw it, and described it as a "very skillful score, with a very skillful libretto." He noted it had been done elsewhere since the premiere, and endorsed it as "a good piece."

There was a problem in that bar sales took a nose dive whenever the opera was done, because for forty minutes of significant time there could not be the usual coming and going and selling of drinks, and ticket prices failed to make up the difference.

In January, president Bolle announced a $1,096,400 budget for 1979, projecting total earned income of $498,306 for the Festival. Contributions amounting to $600,000 were projected, of which $400,000 was anticipated as coming from the general campaign. The board gave unanimous consent to this budget.

In 1978 Darling had put on a Festival of style and substance, and for 1979 he promised more pleasures with *The Merry Widow, The Barber of Seville*, and a double bill of Menotti's *The Medium* and a premiere of a one-act opera by Garland Anderson called *Soyazhe*.

In addition, there would be a stepped-up apprentice program, with a composer-in-residence program, Victorian Salon Recitals, and Opera Memos. The distinguished ACT from San Francisco would come to do Maugham's *The Circle* and Turgenev's *A Month in the Country*. The 1979 brochure emphasized "change—-innovation—-growth—variety" for the Festival. And in November 1979 it was promised *La Traviata* would be done in Denver. In the spring of 1980 there might be a second Denver production, possibly one out of San Francisco, by presumably the Western Opera Theater.

The 1979 theme was "Live From Central City," and it underscored Darling's desire to provide a worthy variety of offerings within a controlled budget.

Curiously few details of staff and casting were to be available until mid-May when full-page ads in the Sunday papers provided them. A number of surprises were at hand. Darling showed the strength of his connections with the San Francisco Opera by bringing in its venerable general director Kurt Herbert Adler to conduct the first five performances of *The Merry Widow* with Mary Costa in the lead. William Francisco would return to direct, with John Conklin doing his first Central City designs.

The *Barber* would revive Robert O'Hearn's 1973 designs with H. Wesley Balk of the Minnesota Opera as director and John Moriarty returning to conduct both Rossini and Menotti. Randall Behr would lead the *Soyazhe* and take over the *Widow* for eight performances.

Darling was busy coordinating, designing, and planning the double bill which he would direct. A May interview with Glenn Giffin made it evident that Darling himself was feeling his work habits threatened by his new responsibilities.

"You're talking," Darling told Giffin," to someone who likes to do things last minute. When I freelanced I went through a period in which I was reluctant to accept that job because I might turn down the perfect Broadway show that was exactly what I wanted to do. With the gray hairs, I have grown to realize that in order to achieve what I want to achieve, it's got to fit into something which can be planned."

Francisco's sense of humor made *The Merry Widow* as funny as the Lubitsch film, and Adler's Viennese background gave the requisite lilt to the music; for Adler the orchestra performed with suavity and verve.

Though Mary Costa was beautiful and acted with skill, she was in poor vocal condition. Howard Hensel was a virile, suave Danilo, and Evelyn Petros was a shining presence as Valencienne.

Francisco's stage direction satirized court etiquette, dalliance, social drinking, money, and the Festival audience. John Conklin's settings had Art Nouveau dazzle. His uses of scrims distanced the action nicely. It was, as I then wrote, "Above all - an excitingly theatrical production. Though its musical, design, and directorial guidance is remarkably unified, it is the sense of a stage being used for fun and frolic that prevails."

The *Barber* was another wholly engaging occasion with great operatic zest. Dominic Cossa's Figaro had immense dash., while Evelyn Petros showed wonderful riches in her mezzo-soprano and in her adamant and comic independence. Gimi Beni, superb as Dr. Bartolo, David Hall, a fresh-voiced Almaviva, and Peter Harrower as Don Basilio completed a strong, balanced cast.

O'Hearn's setting with its louvres and slats, created for the 1973 production, encased the action in an aristocratic world and was one of his most deft. Balk's direction provided the fullest kind of operatic zest, and Moriarty showed exhilarating affection for the music.

*Soyazhe* was a dud, an opera insufficiently analyzed in advance of programming, and did not deserve the expense and effort to produce it. There was much ranting and raving, and the heroine had a 164-measure run of repeating G sharps!

*The Medium* was rare, with Carolyne James a powerful Madame Flora, Maryanne Telese a winsome Monica, and Kevin Anderson was effective as the mute Toby. Darling's direction and setting established a chilling mood for this Grand Guignol piece.

In showing what it meant to be "Live From Central City," Darling provided remarkable riches. Charles Wakefield Cadman's *Shanewis* was done in Williams' Stable, as was *The Picnic* by Richard Cumming, composer- in-residence with the Trinity Square Repertory Theater of Provincetown, Rhode Island, with libretto by Henry Butler who had done the libretto for Marvin David Levy's *Mourning Becomes Electra*, done by the Metropolitan Opera.

Most absorbing of all was Conrad Susa's *Black River*, of which its Act II was done in a workshop presentation, like these other efforts in the Williams Stable. Barbara Brandt, a featured member of the Minnesota Opera and a member of the apprentic faculty, played Pauline L'Allemande, an opera singer who actually sang the first American performance of Delibes's *Lakme*, and went on to a suddenly brilliant European career.

Her later years were wrapped melodramatically in many unsupported legends, but apparently at one time she and her son were detained in a mental institute in Beaver Creek, Wisconsin. Susa's treatment of this intense fabric calls for her to reminisce and fantasize at the institution.

Andrew Porter admired Susa's writing, reporting in *The New Yorker* that the portion performed "displays the flair, liveliness, neatness, and wit that distinguishes his first opera, *Transformations*. It was an imaginative and musically worthy operatic effort."

Again there was *The Face on the Barroom Floor*, and there were all those other things, concerts, recitals, classes for the apprentices going on. In sum, there were four composers-in-residence with works being done. There were great opportunities for the apprentice artists to do many things.

There was good theater too, with a glittering performance of *The Circle* and much of interest in Turgenev's *A Month in the Country* from ACT, though there were but two performances of each, and neither sold out.

Before the end of the Festival it had been announced that the Denver opera productions planned for the following year, *La Traviata* and *The Flying Dutchman*, were canceled, citing fiscal responsibility, long-term fund-raising goals, and a future opera season in Denver as the reason.

Of the $400,000 goal for 1979, about half was raised. There was uncertainty that the balance could be raised before December. Expenses for the Denver operas had been estimated at $116,000 with $55,000 required as support income.

Managing director Kellogg told the press "it is important in the rebuilding of Central City Opera's image as a credible organization that we operate in a fiscally responsible manner. For us to move forward with a fall production at this time, without being totally confident that we can pay for it and cover our normal operating expenses and finish the year in a break-even position, is clearly not in the best interests of the over-all organization."

There had not been any diminishing of the $410,000 indebtedness. The 11 performances of *The Merry Widow*, the six of the *Barber*, and four bills of *The Medium* and *Soyazhe* had done very well at 93% capacity, but for the ACT performances there was only 59% of capacity. Alberta Hunter's two jazz festival performances were sold out.

Kellogg announced a plan to raise funds to insure 1980 at Central City and opera in Denver for the following year." The future of the organization is not nearly so tentative as it was twelve months ago, but if we proceed now with our planned Denver productions, history will repeat itself."

This report was concluded with the earliest-ever announcement for the 1980 Festival of *Cosi Fan Tutte, Candide*, and *The Plough and the Stars*, a new opera by Elie Siegmeister, another offering from the National Opera Institute, from whom *Soyazhe* had come.

In October the Association went to the people of Denver to tell them "The time is Now - The need is critical."

What was needed was $200,000 to pay the summer's bills. Severe nation-wide inflation was at its peak, and regular donors had not made increases in keeping with that rise. There was heavy irony in that the Festival was truly responding to the challenge for fiscal responsibility as well as offering more variety of high quality than ever.

As Kellogg told Giffin, "When people talk about fiscal integrity, if they're talking about our ability to keep our expenses on or under budget, we've done it."

"This time," he continued, "if we don't raise that $200,000 I have very grave doubts - and I can't say it any stronger because that would have to come from the president — that we could continue or mount a season in 1980."

Early in December the board met to hear that the National Endowment for the Arts had given the Association a $125,000 challenge grant to reduce the accumulated deficit, build a cash reserve, and create an endowment. The grant was made on a 3-1 basis, so $375,000 would have to be raised, making a total of $500,000.

Kellogg had told Marjorie Barrett of the Rocky Mountain News in November that "for far too long Central City kept its success and problems 'in house.' They didn't go public. They didn't ask for help. There has been legitimate criticism that Central City for too long was elitist, that a handful of people were 'doing their thing' in the mountains. If there were a deficit at the end of summer, somebody reached into his or her pocket and wrote a check. Those days are long since over. Those people aren't around and even if they were . . . We have had 12 new directors on the board since spring. All of them are hard-nosed financial types. They are enthusiastic about the arts but they are realistic. They are fiscally responsible."

The Association had the problems of the historic properties. Volunteers, willing but untrained, had donated these properties without funds for caretaking. Too many of the repairs were makeshift, and the constant concerns over these properties often made Association managements believe they were museum keepers rather than producers of opera.

By the time of the annual meeting in early December, the Board had raised $230,000 but needed $170,000 more to complete the 1979 fundraising goal. At the same time an award of $10,000 from the National Opera Institute for producing the Siegmeister *Plough and The Stars* in 1980 was announced. Darling received a grant, amount unavailable, to participate in the Institute for Not-For-Profit Management at Columbia University.

On January 23, 1980, the Board accepted a budget of $1.96 million, and approved a Festival program which now offered Leonard Bernstein's *Candide*, *Lucia di Lammermoor*, and Dominick Argenta's *Postcards From Morocco*.

A plan to seek consolidation of indebtedness with one bank or with a consortium of banks was adopted by the Board. A specific timetable was tied to this plan, with a reduction of $107,000 to take place by June 1. In the drive to raise $400,000, $310,000 had been raised.

A gift of $50,000 from the Phipps Foundation matched $50,.000 of the NEA challenge grant, and by March 31, $50,000 would come from Washington. In March it was announced that Atlantic Richfield's ARCO Foundation had made available a $200,000 line of credit, as well as $50,000 for a corporate review by a national management consulting firm.

If a projected $207,000 shortfall in monies due the banks was not reduced by the end of 1980, ARCO would lend the Association $200,000 to pay down the bank's interim financing. That ARCO loan would be repayable July 1982. While an outright gift would have been welcome, this was given a warm greeting.

In March 1980 came word that E. Atwill Gilman, a former president and Board chairman of the Denver Symphony Association, and also a former president of the American Symphony Orchestra League, had been elected chairman of the Board. Gilman had not earlier served on the Central City Opera House Association Board, but his wife, Callae Buell Gilman, daughter of the builder Temple Buell, had served as an honorary director. The problems of arts organizations were familiar to the Gilmans.

There was a new president Marshall Freedman who replaced Bolle. Kellogg hailed Bolle for providing "a style of leadership that has successfully brought together divided interests among our supporters and set us on the track towards our sometimes perilous but nonetheless successfully emerging organizational turnaround."

Amid rumors that there would be no 1980 season unless the banks got their money, ways of rounding up funds were given consideration, and chief among them was the idea of selling off some of the historic properties.

Frank Ricketson was quoted in the *News* by Frances Melrose as feeling that the "new people involved in the project now have no regard for the historical aspects of the Festival. It would be regrettable if the historic properties are sold. They were given for a purpose, and that purpose should be fulfilled. It took a long time to assemble them, and it doesn't seem feasible that they would be sold."

Mary McGlone of the Board believed they were inviolate and that "the guild and the association are under obligation to live up to these trusts. I will fight to the end to retain these properties in fulfillment of the conditions under which they were given and accepted."

Some of these properties were not to be sold, according to stipulations made at the time of giving, Robert Lotito pointed out. Justin Brierly, the Association's first business manager, and then an honorary member without a vote, requested that the Board minutes "register my strong personal protest to the proposed possible sale of the Association's real or personal properties as a possible or potential solution to the Association's present financial dilemma."

The issue had been raised, and would not go away. It was becoming harder and harder to find the money in depth required to keep the Association and Festival going. These properties were costing the Association, and there were nearly forty of them.

The 1980 Festival would take place with 16 performances of *Candide* in the version commissioned by Harold Prince, with Hugh Wheeler's book replacing the original one by Lillian Hellman, and with the highly regarded lyrics of John Latouche, Richard Wilbur, and Stephen Sondheim.

There would be eight performances of *Lucia di Lammermoor*, and five of *Postcards From Morocco*. ACT would come for four performances of Noel Coward's *Hay Fever* and two of Sam Shepard's *Buried Child*. In the composer series there would be *Desire Under the Elms*, by Edward Thomas and Joseph Masteroff from Eugene O'Neill's tragedy, and *Something for the Palace* by Jose Raul Bernardo and Bob Joyner.

The Darling scheme continued as "variety plus." As if there were not enough going on, the apprentices would appear in the 19th century popular success, Heinrich Marschner's *Der Vampyr*.

There was a big lift just prior to the opening of the 1980 Festival. The First National Bank of Denver provided a $316,000 line of credit which enabled the Association to pay $110,000 to three Denver banks, removing from three of the four major historical properties the threat of removal from CCOHA guardianship.

Audiences received a lift from *Candide* which boasted John Mauceri's fine conducting and Peter Mark Schifter's buoyant stage direction and ideal casting. David Eisler's Candide had the right kind of tenor buoyancy and the proper guileless manner, while Claudette Peterson bubbled gloriously as Cunegonde. Joseph McKee sparkled as Voltaire and Dana Krueger made hilarious music with her "I Am So Easily Assimilated." Those familiar with the score missed the "Quiet" and "Eldorado" numbers which were dropped in this production.

For *Lucia*, Janice Hall from Aurora came to conquer with her fresh presence and radiant soprano. Darling designed and directed the production which was unique in the inclusion of a usually excised scene in which Ashton makes a call on Ravenswood with Ashton challenging Ravenswood to a duel.

James Schwisow as Ravenswood, Edgardo of the Italian version, displayed good looks and an agreeable though occasionally forced tenor. David Holloway who had figured in Denver Lyric Opera productions in 1968 and 1969 was a strong Ashton though he imperiled the sheen of his voice by indulging in shouting, in which he was joined by Schwisow. Moriarty led the orchestra in a particularly sensitive reading.

Unquestionably the novelty of the season was *Postcard From Morocco* by Dominic Argento, whose *Colonel Jonathan The Saint* brought havoc to the Denver Lyric Opera in 1971. This cryptic pastiche seemed a sort of *Chorus Line* which promises to be *Casablanca* with characters by Agatha Christie, but goes on to conclude very much like life, a very baffling but intriguing affair, given a performance of high style.

John Mauceri led seven instrumentalists in a deft rendition which held the mark of authority in Mauceri's leadership. He had conducted the much admired performance by the Opera Society of Washington, D.C., and both performances had the same stage director, Lou Galterio, as well as the same stylish designer, Zack Brown.

Claudette Peterson gleamed while Barbara Hocher intrigued as The Lady With the Cake Box. Barry McCauley, William Dansby now recovered from the vocal problems of Lucia, Michael Best, and Wayne Turnage all were excellent singing actors.

The threat implied in August 1979 when managing director Peter Kellogg urged on the Association the need for fiscal responsibility came home to the Association at the end of September when Kellogg resigned, saying "I've always been intrigued by 11th hour crises, and felt that any expertise I may have lies in handling these challenges. With Central City, the job, as I saw it, was to take Central City off a survival mode and into a creative management mode. I think we have made great strides in that direction."

In November it was announced that Ann Farris Darling, wife of the artistic director, would become managing director, coming from her post as executive director of Opera America in Washington. She told the press that she and Robert, whose contract was renewed, had had a lengthy talk in which he said, "you know, we mustn't forget what the original mission of this organization was; it was the Central City Opera House Association, not the Central City Opera Association. That says to me," she continued," that there must be an interrelation between Central City and the properties there and art."

She went out of her way to commend Peter Kellogg for his "determination to find a way to keep this organization going for the last three years - and by God, it was just dogged determination-I'm not sure this organization would be alive today. That guy had guts, that's all I can say. And I really admire him for it."

She had worked as administrative assistant to Kurt Herbert Adler at the San Francisco Opera, as a management trustee for the American Guild of Musical Artists, best known as AGMA, in its Pension and Welfare Fund, and as production director for the theater at Wolf Trap Farm Park, across the Potomac from Washington, D.C., and for Expo '67 in Montreal.

She had indeed a wealth of experience which president Marshall Freedman recognized, and hailed. She had worked in management production, labor relations, government relations, and fund-raising. She was indeed "one of the most highly respected opera administrators in America," according to Freedman. And she kept her presence charming and vivacious.

The Boettcher Foundation greeted the new managing director a week later with a $50,000 historic preservation grant, to be followed by a $60,000 challenge grant to be matched 1-1; the Colorado Historical Society matched the $50,000 grant with another $50,000.

At the annual meeting in mid-December, the Johnson Foundation pledged $25,000 to make a total of $331,000 towards the $375,000 goal. Early in February it was announced that the 1980 goal had been attained, which meant that one-third of the 1981 budget of $1,100,000 had been raised, and this was the most ever raised in an annual campaign. This also enabled the Association to qualify for its annual portion of the $125,000 National Endowment Challenge.

In mid-February the 1981 Festival season was announced. There would be yet another revival of *The Ballad of Baby Doe* which had been consistently successful in each of its three revivals. There would be *Madama Butterfly* and a new opera, *Fables*, by Hugh Aitken, with 16 performances of *Baby Doe*, 12 of the Puccini melodrama, and five of the new work.

Good news continued to roll out from the Association office. A commitment to winter opera in Denver was made. There would be a single production in 1982, two in 1983, three in 1984, and four in 1985 and 1986.

Financial planning was being done in advance,"for the project will result in a budget increase of approximately $250,000 for the first year, funds for which will be raised from sources not currently used to support Association activities in Central City."

"One of the reasons we can finally launch this effort," Gilman told the press, "is because it will have the rigid, detailed financing it needs - the planning that is even more urgent than ever today because of rising costs of inflation."

Ann Darling was quoted as saying of grand opera in Denver, "We think it is most important. It will allow Central City to stabilize its operations on a year- round basis, to build a solid staff. We think it will serve the summer season better. We have an expanding arts public. We will produce grand opera in Denver. We cannot do that in Central City. It is not appropriate in the opera house. The audience wants both - the small chamber opera and grand opera. The potential audience is here. We now have solid Central City support. It needs building. We think that one will feed on the other."

A special committee, the Resources Planning Group's Winter Opera Committee, with board members and Robert and Ann Darling would prepare a detailed five-year plan for winter opera in Denver through 1986.

Two staff additions were made in March, with J. Glen Arko as Director of Development and Barbara Chidester as Marketing Director. Later in March, Charles T. Leasure, president of Channel 9- KBTV, was named board president succeeding Freedman.

The traditional *Baby Doe* was going to be done by a new team, conductor John Moriarty and stage director Peter Mark Schifter, neither of whom had ever seen the work produced. This turned out fortuitous, for Moriarty illuminated musical details from a fresh perspective, catching the high drama of the work with vibrant feeling. Schifter paced with energy for a rare synthesis of music and drama.

Karen Hunt was considered by Edwin Levy, co-director of the original production, to be the best of all the Baby Does he had seen and heard. She was clarion-voiced, with noble enunciation, and excellent dramatic comprehension. She made particular dramatic point of the Windsor Hotel scene with its "Ladies with their heads held high," and there was lustre in all the arias, especially the concluding one.

Handsome, stalwart William Justus was a good Tabor though he did tend to scowl his way through the role. Not any more than a number of others could Dana Krueger erase memories of Frances Bible's Augusta. Krueger was adequate but could not manage seeming disagreeable or to control her upper voice.

*Madama Butterfly* was a popular success. Darling, who designed and directed the production, went for its melodrama without stint but with delicacy. There was strength and musical sensitivity in Randall Behr's conducting.

Although there was considerable sheen in Martha Sheil's singing, everything was done at the same loud level, the least delicate aspect of the production. James Schwisow was back in a large-scaled performance as Pinkerton, exactly right dramatically as the immature lad being undone by the fragile, fragrant Japan of old.

A less realistic production than Darling's would have been more interesting, but he worked close to the sense of the Belasco melodrama, seeking firm, theatrical ground.

*Fables* turned out to be one of the nicest surprises in years, an unexpected delight. With no more than five performances, it never did build strong support although it was a critical triumph. After the season many realized they had missed a treat.

The sourcebook was LaFontaine's moralistic tales, ten being utilized by author-composer Hugh Aitken. The audience laughed merrily, relishing the amusement derived from mankind's follies. The music, with echoes of Couperin, Rameau, and Lully, was enchanting. Peter Mark Schifter set the high visual tone of the production as well as an emphasis on ironic humor.

The vocal pieces spoofed French classical opera with elaborate lines carried to absurd lengths, always set nicely for the voices. Henry Mollicone's conducting explored the music for its point and humor. Lowell Detweiler's sets and costumes came out of Watteau in highly imaginative style.

There were only four in the cast, Pamela South, Peter Strummer, Anthony Laciura, and Ken Scown, each of whom tripled in roles. Memorable moments offered soprano

South as a furiously knitting ant in conversation with the vain grasshopper, so well done by Scown, and Strummer as the vainest of all, the crow seduced by flattery. Laciura was the very shrewd fox who got the cheese.

As had come to be expected from Darling, the Festival Extras were distinctive. *The Face on the Barroom Floor* seemed to have become a permanent fixture despite concern on some parts that the bar was prevented from earning larger sums in the dispensation of drink.

Composers at Central City this year included Charles Strouse, composer of *Annie* and *Bye,Bye Birdie*, who was finishing up and overseeing *The Nightingale*, a version of the familiar Hans Christian Anderson tale, and Frank Lewin working on *Burning Bright* from the Steinbeck work.

The apprentice artists gala consisted of *The Mistake* by composer Jonathan Sheffer and author Stephen Wadsworth, dealing with dreadful events following a singer's memory lapse. This was followed by Offenbach's *The Isle of Tulipatan*, brightly staged by Michael Ehrman, with John Moriarty as musical director, and Jean Glennon of Denver as the foppish prince. Finally there was Lee Hoiby's *The Scarf* staged by Darling and led by Duain Wolfe.

The variety in the Olios is suggested by one program which consisted of an aria from Mascagni's *Iris*, a song from Stephen Sondheim's *Pacific Overtures*, a duet from Carlisle Floyd's *Susannah*, a duet from Robert Ward's *The Lady from Colorado*, and Mussorgsky's "The Song of the Flea."

There was no diminution of effort, although it had not been possible for Conrad L. Susa to return to continue work in Central City on his opera about Lola Montez.

Many who had not attended the operas and had been otherwise involved did attend the annual jazz festival late in August when 13 Dixieland jazz bands, five ragtime pianists, and gospel singer Sippie Wallace took part in events all over town.

There had been many contented audiences, so when the Boettcher Foundation presented a gift of $100,000 for general operations and restoration of historic properties, it seemed bliss was ahead.

The Association reported in a newly devised newsletter that 22,676 tickets to events in Central City had been sold, with the opera house 88.2 per cent sold out for the entire Festival. There had been a 26 per cent rise in subscriptions over 1980, and a remarkable increase in group sales since 1980 of over 281 per cent. By November it was reported that 44 per cent of the goal of $800,000 or $348,000 had been raised.

Sales of Festival tickets in all categories were noted, and overall opera tickets were up 50.9 per cent over 1980.

In personal correspondence from Darling in October 1981, he wrote that "we are now planning for the 1982 50th anniversary Season. If all goes well, it will pull together many dear hopes, desires, and goals the Association has cherished for a number of years."

There was good news in the matching of the $125,000 National Endowment Challenge Grant. That it even exceeded this goal, by 77%, was truly impressive. By this time, over 47 per cent of the annual campaign had been reached.

On December 15, Gilman expressed himself satisfied with this effort to face the "tremendous challenges" of the future.

"The time for studies is over. The time for action is now," he concluded.

Nothing would stand still, however. The fire department had set up new fire regulations in the opera house which required removal of 47 seats to make emergency clearance possible. This cost the Association something like $1,500 per performance.

The $500,000 debt had been reduced by a $28,000 payment to Metro Bank of Denver, but there were $100,000 in pledges which could not be collected in the present economy.

Darling had been a leader in getting the Board together to fuse its energies, and a two-day retreat was held to plan the next quarter century.

Everyone contributed to this think session, but it all came back to the properties. Could they be leased? Could they be developed in cooperation with a company? Should they be sold outright? Whatever was done should be done in 1982. And the options seemed seriously limited.

The Association should become self-sufficient within ten years, and up-to-date budget practices should be brought into operation. All-year-round use of the opera house and development of the Teller House as a first-class hotel were further recommendations.

The overriding message of this session was Gilman's: "Let's bite the bullet now."

This campaign was to have concluded on December 31, 1981, but the goal of $525,000 was short $17,854.

At the Founder's Day gathering on January 27, 1982, Dr. Ronald Tegtmeier celebrated the founders' vision as he developed the theme, "proud of our past and excited about our future."

On February 1, Gilman and Ann Darling attended a luncheon given by the Gannett Foundation at which she accepted a check for the Association, but the next day her resignation was announced, in what was described as a disagreement over long-range planning and finances.

She told Glenn Giffin, "I won't deny it. It is terribly with regret but I have resigned. The executive committee has been having to wrestle with many difficulties - and I obviously thoroughly understand them."

"Under the current financial situation, the Board is operating under terrible constraints, and I appreciate that. But we do have certain differences, and I feel, therefore, that it's not a situation when my talents can be put to their best use. And thus, I've really decided it's time for me to go elsewhere."

According to Giffin, Gilman had not known of the resignation, though he did know of "some conditions that, if they weren't met, she felt she couldn't continue."

On February 6 came the ominous threat that had not before been spoken soberly, that on February 23 the Board would meet to decide whether or not to observe the 1982 Festival. The "terrible constraints" Ann Darling had spoken of were real, and that reality of $640,000 had led to Central City's being turned down by the Helen K. and Arthur Johnson Foundation and the Coors Foundation, as no plan to remove that debt had been put into operation.

J. Glen Arko, the Association's Director of Development was quoted by Frances Melrose in the News as saying "we want to clear out the debt of $640,000 which has accumulated in bits over a ten-year period. This is no disrespect to Ann Darling. She kept costs down tremendously. But we must now start forward funding for a 1983 season. We will not spend more than we can raise in ticket prices or earned income."

More sobering talk from president Charles Leasure was quoted in the News, "Our financial obligation must be met at the expense of some or all of the artistic programs for a year."

Arko thought it was a "50-50 matter" whether there would be a 1982 Festival. Given the downbeat comments of the crucial parties, it appeared that what needed doing on February 23 was to formalize the decision to go dark.

In Arko's declaration that "I've never seen such a rallying round of board members and Central City supporters as I've witnessed in the last 48 hours. They're all optimistic that we will pull through" there was a positive attitude.

There appeared not to have been any talk about Robert Darling's future. His budgets had been approved by the board throughout his years and suddenly he was out. His leadership had been rich in imagination and financial responsibility.

Carrick Hill was to head an interim committee that would manage the Association's business, substituting for Ann Darling.

*The Denver Post* editorialized that "This is one element of Colorado's cultural life too valuable to lose," explaining that taxes and the smallness of the opera house were the cause of the financial crunch.

The other shoe was dropped February 24 when the Board, on motion from Carrick Hill of the Transition Committee, voted to cancel the 1982 Festival and take four steps. The overriding information was that the interest on the $640,000 debt would have an annual cost of $125,000.

As rough as was the decision to cancel for 1982, it was a recognition that an inescapable biting of the bullet must take place, and that the move was justified. Hereafter monies would be raised in advance of a season, contrary to Anne Evans' belief that it was important for public support to be declared annually, and before the season. From now on there would be a financial stability never before in evidence.

There was heavy irony in that the Five Year Plan, worked on in December at the retreat, had been completed just as the decision to skip a season was made. Though inoperative during 1982, the plan was nevertheless considered to be functioning, "just 90 days off the timetable."

The heart of this significant plan was the ordering of flow, of seeing to it that decisions were on target, that a strategy of "getting the tracks to merge" would be held to.

Normally, planning for summer 1982 would have been completed in February, but as it stood, decisions for summer 1983 would be made in September 1982, and a fund drive would begin in June 1982.

There was little doubt that the problem of raising money to pay for the previous Festival drew upon energies that would have been better utilized in advance of a season. As summer drew near, it became clear action was required.

In February four steps had been seen as obligatory. First was the sale of such properties as the Chain O' Mines Hotel, the Knights of Pythias Building, and outlying houses unused for the housing of Festival personnel. Secondly, a campaign to raise $1.5 million for "forward funding" must be initiated; thirdly, the staff must be cut in size, and fourth, advanced planning for 1983 should be done as soon as possible.

There was as well a new problem in that the University of Denver, now beset with its own financial distress, a problem stemming from the same economic downturn in Denver that had caused upheaval for the Association, was no longer capable of carrying the liability of obviously deteriorating structures. The insurance was about to leap from $12,500 annually to nearly $47,000.

These issues were brought home sharply with word that the back wall of the opera house required reinforcing at a cost of $78,000.

There was a small but highly intense debate in the columns of *The Denver Post* between Glenn Giffin who claimed the decision to cancel "smacks of haste and panic rather than the sort of deliberation boards are supposed to make" and At Gilman who responded to say that "serious and prolonged consideration had been given by the executive committee - certainly there was no 'panic'."

Among the debts were $240,000 owed to Columbia Savings and Loan on a mortgage of the Teller House, and $200,000 to the Bank of America on a consolidation of smaller loans. In 1981, $200,000 was borrowed from the then First of Denver to cover losses of $52,000 for the jazz festival and $36,000 for *Fables*.

Something did need to be done to give Central City supporters a lift, so the United Bank of Denver volunteered to sponsor a benefit 50th anniversary at the Boettcher Concert Hall on August 14.

Frank Guarrera would come as Master of Ceremonies, and John Moriarty and Carl Topilow, conductor of the Colorado Philharmonic Orchestra, the orchestra of the occasion, would share conducting duties.

Singers included those who had sung at Central City: Janice Hall, Michael Devlin, J. Patrick Raftery, Vinson Cole, Barry McCauley, and Martha Sheil. A delegation came from the Aspen Music Festival, and Sheri Greenawald represented the Santa Fe Opera. Many others were asked to come but declined.

Governor Lamm of Colorado, Mayor McNichols of Denver, and Mayor Russell of Central City joined to declare August 14 through 21 as Central City Festival Week.

The gala raised $57,000, and did get the Association a small amount of publicity.

On August 20, sale of the Chain O'Mines Hotel, the Knights of Pythias Building, and the Bank Building to Community Services Collaborative of Boulder was reported sold "for not less than $450,000," actually $495,000. A 30-year lease of the Teller House was included in the transaction.

When the Board met to approve the sale, of 39 members 32 were present. There was but one negative vote.

It was also reported that an operating budget of $303,000 had been raised, and $64,000 had been placed in escrow towards "forward funding" for the 1983 Festival. A drive to raise $186,000 in unrestricted funds to complete the $250,000 "forward funding" for 1983 was to be launched.

In short order this good news was followed by announcement that John Moriarty would become Artistic Director, and that Duain Wolfe would be Artistic Administrator, planning the 1983 Festival.

# THE MORIARTY YEARS

The Central City Opera had survived yet another crisis, and the momentous fact was that forward funding would henceforth be observed. No more would the Board spend the winter catching up with the losses of the previous season. Anne Evans had been right in her time, but in a world of flow charts and balance options, that old policy had gone.

Gilman's words that "We are looking forward to continuation of outstanding performances for the next 50 years" were good to hear, and John Moriarty was the one who would carry out policies that would insure that this would be the case.

In the fall of 1982, potential donors were told it cost "$31,000 for each opera performance, and that the maximum ticket sales of the 750 seats was $11,000," leaving a balance of $20,000 to be raised for each performance. There would have to be consideration of higher ticket prices but it was not believed that this was the time.

The theme continued as before,"Funding the Future while Preserving the Past."

A new outlook was in evidence. Word came that the Chain O' Mines Hotel would become the Golden Rose Hotel, offering such latter day necessaries as hot tubs and saunas, along with "Victorian baths of marble, porcelain and brass." It apparently was going to be possible to escape television, though a "relaxation room" with films, library, and games promised some diversion.

Across the way in the Bank Building, rooms were being renovated, some of them as housekeeping apartments to be operated in conjunction with The Golden Rose.

There was good news in the matching of the $125,000 National Endowment Challenge Grant. That it even exceeded this goal by 77 per cent was truly impressive. By this time over 47 per cent of the annual campaign had been reached. On December 15, Gilman expressed himself satisfied with this effort to face the "tremendous challenges" of the future.

By mid-January the Association had exceeded its goal by about $30,000, having raised $585,393, 24 per cent above that raised in 1981; a further $676,000 was gathered in for restricted programs.

In March, ticket orders went out over the name of the new president, Carrick Hill, Gilman now having become Chairman rather than carrying both titles as during 1982. Hill had moved back to Denver to set himself up in business after leaving The Denver and New York City. He urged patrons to make a 20 per cent increase in donations over the previous year.

In April, casting and staff appointments were announced. *La Traviata* would be done for 15 performances while *The Elixir of Love* would receive ten performances. The Verdi would open the season July 9 and close it on August 5.

John Moriarty would conduct *La Traviata* which Michael Ehrman, Acting Coach for the Apprentice Program in 1981, would direct, with Richard Seger as designer. Seger was resident scenic designer for ACT in San Francisco.

Duain Wolfe would conduct the Donizetti with stage direction by William Francisco who had brought such merriment to the 1978 *Don Pasquale* and the 1979 *The Merry Widow*, on Harry Feiner's designs. Feiner was assistant professor of theater at the University of Missouri, and designed for Missouri Repertory Theater.

Francisco now taught theater at Wesley University at Middletown, Connecticut, and Ehrman since 1980 had been stage director for Texas Opera Theater, and had spent the winter of 1982-83 in Paris as assistant to Peter Brook on his controversial *Carmen*, which dispensed with big choruses and used a cast of eight performers.

The balance was on the side of academic talents, not on practiced professional qualifications.

Not much was known of the announced casts. Violettas were Karen Huffstodt and Marilyn Brustradt, while Alfredos were to be Frank Farina, a 1981 apprentice, and Peter Puzzo, with John Brandstetter and George Massey as elder Germonts.

For the Donizetti, Pamela South, who had won much attention in *Fables* would sing Adina, with Tonio DiPaolo as Nemorino, Robert Orth as Belcore, and Jan Oppalach as Dulcamara.

Sixteen apprentice artists were announced, and a group of ten Studio Singers in the 20-25 age group who thus were less experienced than the 23-29 year old apprentices, would be given special training.

Early in May, Moriarty was heard being interviewed by KVOD's John Wolfe, declaring that "Central City was back with a vengeance," that the "lights were green," and that the future of Central City looked "very good - back on the center of the track."

Recitals by the apprentice artists and scenes by the younger Opera Studio Singers were matters he touched on. The apprentices would play lesser roles in the Verdi, and would serve as understudies.

Best of all, Moriarty continued, was a "return to the past," to doing the "old repertory in a new style." He thought the Donizetti would be like nothing ever seen in Central

City, and would be a wonderful show. "A spirit of fun and excitement" should settle in on Central City in 1983.

The day before the re-opening at Central City the *Rocky Mountain News* carried the banner headline "Rescue Brought Future for Opera - 'Atwill Saves Us' Unofficial Slogan for Central City's 2nd 50 years."

Gilman was credited in Keith Raether's story with leading the drive to resolve the financial crisis so that the Association might enter the 1983 Festival with debts retired and $250,000 in the bank towards the new season's expenses. Fifty years later it seemed to be proved that opera at Central City was here to stay, and the Evans policy had been reversed to accommodate the economics of the day.

Opera was coming to Denver. And although Central City now would have no finger in Denver opera, it was part of its history. Nathaniel Merrill's advance work prepared the way, finding some money and much energy for opera at Boettcher Concert Hall where the first splashy season opened in April 1983 with Placido Domingo in *La Boheme* and James MacCracken, who had made his professional debut at Central City, as Otello in Verdi's masterpiece. The framework for opera at Central City was altered for all time.

For the Festival program Moriarty had written "Now in 1983 we are at yet another time of revival and renewal," making reference to the earlier hiatus which ended in 1946 after World War II.

"We look back to the 40s and 50s when stability and continuity of leadership ensured artistic growth," he continued, "and we discover that high standards of production and performance did not mean that opera had to be lacking in fun for audience and performers. Indeed, Central City taught the world that opera need not be a stodgy affair in order to be good . . . Although our spirit reaches back three or four decades, it is youthful in its outlook. And that is only appropriate for this company which has always been known for its youthful vitality, as well as its artistic excellence."

It was curious that Moriarty spoke in the News of being ready "to return Central City to the position it held in the 50s," a time devoted to implementation of ambitions, gratifying in the success of *The Ballad of Baby Doe* and the sophisticated delights of *La Perichole* though flawed by problems with *Carmen* and *Ariadne auf Naxos* as its ambitions were pressed. What really set the highest standards were the late 40s work by St. Leger-Cooper-Oenslager and the early 60s work by Merrill and O'Hearn. What Moriarty really meant was the reestablishment of the national prominence Central City once held.

Moriarty thought 1983 was a "trial year," in the sense that "we have to re-establish credibility with the business community. They want to know if we can live within our means."

"Opera is a very expensive animal -" Moriarty continued, "as a rule of thumb the box office only covers a third of operation costs. But we're already planning the '84 season. We're in this for the duration."

And Moriarty's commitment was made complete. He purchased a house in Central City, the McGlone house.

Recognizing the Central City past for what it was, and giving emphasis to his wish for "Central City to be a place where young singers can develop their skills to the fullest, along with maintenance of the house's reputation for innovation in production," Moriarty was clearly very much caught up in the town and the opera house.

He told the News's Keith Raether *La Traviata* would be done in a "standard romantic interpretation," but promised that "artistic liberties will be taken with *Elixir*."

The 1983 Festival was budgeted at $712,812, with a total 1983 fiscal budget of $1,163,460, a budget that could be compared favorably with the 1980 budget of $1,096,000.

A projection of $247,000 in performance income was made, based on 15 performances of the Verdi, and ten of the Donizetti. By mid-July with three weeks to go, the Association had taken in $195,000.

So, on Saturday evening, July 9, opera again made a return to Central City. Tuxedos and elegant gowns filled the Teller House and the walk to the Opera House. The newly refurbished Teller House, spruced up at a reputed cost of $300,000, drew admiration. According to the *Post*'s Pat Collins, who as in earlier days covered society activities on a scale larger than that in which the operatic events were reported, some 383 first-nighters paid $200 per couple for cocktails, opera, dinner, and dancing.

On stage, with a conviction moving to behold, with the individuality of Central City maintained, was a musically and theatrically splendid production of *La Traviata*.

Karen Huffstodt was the opening night Violetta, a beauty with abundant vocal and dramatic talents. She drew on impressive vocal resources for a completely felt and expressed interpretation. Far more subtlety than in the usual elder Germont was present in John Brandstetter's superb offering. Peter Puzzo was earnest rather than ardent as Alfredo.

Michael Lehrman's stage direction concentrated stylishly on pivotal relationships, while his sense of detail in establishing character was impressive. Richard Seger's setting, with triple arches as principal elements, variously used with flair in the different scenes, was admirable, as was the attention to flooring painting with gilt and purple to establish the glitter of the milieu.

The alternate was another beauty, Marilyn Brustadt, who made a strong impression. Frank Farina, the 1981 apprentice who now called himself "Franco," was a steadily expressive Alfredo with a fine tenor. In 1990 he joined The Met. George Massey as Pere Germont was undone by a metallic voice in forte passages and superficial acting.

Moriarty had promised novelty for *The Elixir of Love* and no one was let down in this rambunctious production, directed with giddy comic sense by William Francisco, with the surprising pleasures of Harry Feiner's contemporary-styled settings which suited its impudent manner.

Tonio di Paolo took audiences for his own with the firm beauty of his tenor as well as with his impish comic sense. Pamela South had shown her wit in *Fables* and her dramatic fire and spunky soprano in Opera Colorado's *La Boheme*, and now she showed pure and brilliant coloratura singing.

Robert Orth played Sergeant Belcore as part vainglorious warrior and part lame-brained baton-twirler who happened to have a superb baritone. Jan Opalach as the fake pharmacist Dulcamara was an amiable rogue with a rich bass baritone.

In his initial conducting stint at Central City, Duain Wolfe showed a new side of his musical authority in the exuberance of orchestral playing.

During the first week of the Festival it was announced that the Association's Historic Properties Development Committee proposed using these properties as the basis for an endowment.

In September the 1984 season was announced. There would be *Rigoletto* and *La Cenerentola*, which was being called "Cinderella," and *The Student Prince*, which would play in Denver at Loretto Heights College Theater and in Fort Collins and Colorado Springs.

Casting moved ahead, and in November it was announced that Sheryl Woods, who had gained prestige when she had at a moment's notice taken over for Noelle Rogers in Santa Fe Opera's production of Rossini's *Le Comte Ory*, would sing Gilda with David Holloway, a Central City chorus alumnus, to sing Rigoletto. Stephanie Friede, another former apprentice, would sing Cinderella. There would be another old friend Dominic Cossa, back as Dr. Engel in *The Student Prince*.

Paul Powers became president of the Board at the annual meeting in December, and he expressed the hope that *The Student Prince* would help broaden the financial base through its tour. Powers told the meeting, "I can envision Central City becoming an arts mecca for this region, like Santa Fe."

The big news however was that the Central City Opera House Association now was in the black, with "forward funding" in excess of $74,330.

The musicians had felt pushed aside in these recent years of crisis, and their assertion of rights threatened yet another tempest. The Denver Musicians Association asked that a federal judge prevent the Central City Opera House Association from hiring non-union musicians, a provision of the contract in use. After three weeks' negotiations out-of-court the Association agreed to honor the existing contract. At the same time the likewise disgruntled stagehands threatened action. The musicians agreed to stay neutral in the face of such an action.

Already the musical atmosphere of Denver was becoming less tense. The emergence of Opera Colorado had unnerved some supporters of Central City who believed Merrill was staging a revenge action in turn for his 1972 dismissal. Others doubted Denver's ability to support two major opera companies in their midst.

Moriarty went out of his way to differentiate the two companies, and to state that "any artistically successful opera helps us." The coming years were to show how going to the opera nurtured further appreciation. Success in Central City would feed on success for Denver's Opera Colorado.

It should not have been a surprise that in a way the 1984 *Rigoletto* was a reprise of 1974; Sheryl Woods's Gilda was a total delight and former apprentice David Holloway's Rigoletto had elemental power. Evan Bortnick was yet another Duke unable to master applause for his "La donna mobile," and otherwise graceless.

With Peter Strummer and Robert Orth heading the cast, Rossini's *La Cenerentola* proved completely engaging. Gran Wilson's introduction to Central City as a youthfully handsome, pleasing light tenor, was very welcome, and Stephanie Friede was a winsome Cinderella. Jeffrey Wells was an imposing as well as light-hearted Alidoro; his promise was fulfilled in his going to The Met in 1988. Robert Baustian conducted a merry if sometimes casual performance.

Stage director Theodore Pappas took the cliches of Romberg's *The Student Prince* very lightly. Keith Olsen, who by 1990 would sing the Italian Tenor in the San Francisco Opera production of the Strauss *Capriccio*, sang Prince Karl Franz. Peter Strummer had a speaking role in which he seemed to improvise from moment to moment. Dominic Cossa singing "Golden Days" enlivened the hoary material. Those who loved it simply loved it. Duain Wolfe conducted with flair. On tour it was disappointingly attended.

Just before the end of the season, Sheryl Woods, Dominic Cossa, Stephanie Friede, and apprentice singer Don Bernardini were heard in an evening of opera pops.

It was during a Saturday evening performance of *La Cenerentola* that plaster hurled down from the elaborately painted ceiling to hit four people sitting near the far left aisle, bruising them as well as frightening the entire audience.

In 1983 the Association had received $30,000 in federal aid for renovation of walls, foundations, and the electrical system, all of which at the time seemed a more urgent need than the ceiling. A sagging rear wall and the erosion of foundations by the stream flowing beneath the opera house were clearly problems of dangerous possibilities.

A plan was being developed for repair of the flume carrying the water and to divert all underground water.

But the major concern was immediate, and that was to restore the ceiling to safety and to its original beauty. The $80,000 cost of a new roof would be shared equally by Bill Gossard, the 1987 chairman emeritus of the Association, and by the El Pomar Foundation of Colorado Springs. The $60,00 cost of restoration of the ceiling was borne by the Stanton Foundation, set up by Ed Stanton, husband of the late May Bonfils.

This extended process was not completed until just before the 1987 season opening, when there was universal delight in the achievement, which restored accurately the original 1878 designs of John C. Massman, the San Francisco artist-designer.

The process was immensely complicated. Under floodlights, photographs of all details were made. Some dozen samples of the art work were carved out of the ceiling in five-foot segments, and transported to the Denver studio of Grammar of Ornament. The color studies were intensive so that the true tints could be found. A great many overpaintings over the years made this difficult. On 16-foot square canvas panels the designs were painted, then applied to wooden frames to be attached to the ceiling, for easier repair in case of need.

By this time opera finances were well controlled. Production costs were about $70,000 below the $1.3 million annual budget, yet $700,000 more would be needed to break even. The debt would be more than $100,000. The tours to Colorado Springs, Fort Collins, and Denver had generated no more than $10,000.

Two productions were promised for 1985, *Carmen* and *The Desert Song*, while a third production would be performed if the $700,000 were raised. The big news was the increase in ticket sales, $375,000 for 1984, a far cry from the $260,000 for 1983.

By late January, $772,000 had been raised in donations for the 1985 season, and it turned out that instead of being $70,000 under budget in production funds, the figure was $126,000. This meant that for three years in a row opera was in the black. Because of this it was possible to announce that a third opera would be given, and that it would be Donizetti's *The Daughter of the Regiment*.

Bill Gossard now was president, succeeding Paul Powers. A former rancher in the Craig area, he had served from 1960 until 1968 in the Colorado House of Representatives, and at this time he was a member of the Metropolitan Opera National Council. His wife Carol had been active in the Colorado Council on the Arts and Humanities.

By early February Daniel Rule, former managing director of the New York City Opera, had come aboard as the new general manager.

Rule told me when he came how he had gotten a full experience in opera in New York."Everybody did a little of everything in those days, the early 60s - it was like a family thing - everybody did what had to be done." Initially he had worked on logistics - the problems of getting people, scenery, costumes, and the orchestra to the right place at the right time - and this was for him a fine education in the mechanics of an opera house. His schooling had made him superbly qualified.

*Carmen* was a well-meant effort which lacked a Carmen who was passionately involved. Valerie Waters possessed a fatal reserve which prevented a consistent focus on the role. Jerrold Norman did not have the voice to do justice to Don Jose's great aria. Joyce Guyer showed the lovely singing which took her to The Met in 1988. Wayne Turnage appealed as Escamillo. Deidra Palmour sparkled as Mercedes, and many thought she would have been an exciting Carmen, a role she did perform for the Youth Performance. John Moriarty conducted a vivid performance.

Donizetti's *The Daughter of the Regiment* was a delight, and remarkable in featuring a Marie who was eight-months into her pregnancy. Sheryl Woods enchanted with her vocal assurance and the lightness of her acting, and above all in the purity of her soprano. Gran Wilson handled his lyric tenor deftly. Peter Strummer showed his grand comic gifts, and Jan Curtis was hilarious as the Marquise. Francis Cullinan's stage direction was vivacious and Mark Flint exacted a fine musical performance from soloists, chorus, and orchestra.

*The Desert Song* proved Moriarty's case - that American operetta was charming. Erich Parce as the double-faced lead brought immense vocal appeal and wit in his acting to make this a funny and melodious production. Sarah Rice was a convincing Margot, and everyone was handsome or pretty on this stage. Theodore Pappas exuded great humor and charm in this production, while Duain Wolfe made the Romberg score one to relish.

Early in August it was disclosed that ticket sales were $70,000 over the 1984 season, and at the annual meeting it was reported that productions were $40,000 under budget. There had been a 22 per cent increase in ticket sales over 1984, for a 91 per cent capacity.

By then announcement of the 1986 season could be made. It would offer *La Boheme* with Don Bernardini as Rodolfo, Robert Orth as Figaro in *The Barber of Seville*, and Victor Herbert's *Naughty Marietta*.

After six years of attending to Central City's financial problems, Atwill Gilman resigned as chairman, an action which moved Bill Gossard into that position while J. Landis Martin became president.

No one had been particularly excited by the idea of yet another *Boheme* but when Maryanne Telese joined voice with Don Bernardini it became irresistible. A strong company, including Erich Parce as Marcello, Peter Strummer as Benoit, and Andrew Wentzel as Colline, found a fresh attitude towards this familiar work and the surprise was exhilarating. John Moriarty's conducting was just right and Michael Ehrman's stage direction found a tender emotional tone.

The *Barber* was a big hit. Director Lou Galterio found a comic brilliance in the work, and his fail-proof cast delivered with polish and spontaneity. Robert Orth was a masterful comic as Figaro, and Stella Zambalis as Rosina was delectable in voice as well as beauty. Carroll Freeman was an outstanding Almaviva, while Dr. Bartolo was ideal for Peter Strummer. Kenneth Bell gave a funny and strong Basilio. Galterio's comic imagination matched the effervescence of Mark Flint's conducting.

Zack Brown's production was typical of the productions being done at Central City. At their best as in this, there was a breezy regard for reality. Zack Brown's banner-like drop cloths had no more substance than the plots but they never got in the way of the action, and provided an apt abandonment to charm.

Without dramatic relevance, Victor Herbert's *Naughty Marietta* is simply silly, but Herbert's melodies help one when impatience seems to grab the elbow. Cecily Nall was a bright Marietta and Michael Ballam a stalwart hero with a strong baritone. The songs were applauded but the spirit of the work is not for today.

There remained $147,481 to raise to meet the 1986 budget of $1.2 million. Martin observed, "It is not enough to break even; if we don't end up with a surplus of $50,000 to $100,000 this year, our task next year (raising funds under the new tax laws) will be nearly impossible."

Bill Gossard added, "The general economic malaise has cost Central City a diminution of its normal level of giving. We hope - and urge - that everyone will actually give more this year in anticipation of the tax law change."

Ticket revenues were at a high of $465,506, with 95 per cent of capacity filled. The activity was so infectiously healthy that Atwill Gilman, who had retired in April for health reasons, was back as chairman with Martin as president.

Meanwhile efforts to restore the damaged ceiling were continuing, and on Saturday, June 27, a "first viewing" was set. The revelation of artistic restoration was breathtaking. As Mary Chandler wrote in the *News*, "The new Renaissance revival ceiling cheers like a swirl of whipped cream. Lyres in azure form the corners with golden medallions between; the center, or oculus, like a spyglass gazing into the Central City sky, is painted in 'trompe l'oeil' fashion with pink and white clouds scudding along a field of blue."

The opera house had now arrived at an almost incomparable elegance. There were always complaints about the seats, those kitchen chairs fastened together to make them unmoveable, but with history inscribed on their backs. There were times when a neighbor's flesh was equally resistant. Velvet cushions had been added to ease the stress. Never were there enough complaints to bring change.

Other major improvements had been made. The rear wall was reinforced. The auditorium was rewired, the ceiling replaced and redecorated, the lobby spruced up. A new light board and theatrical lighting system was past due.

In November at the annual meeting, Duain Wolfe relayed Moriarty's dominant ideas, these being that "the Central City Opera was on the threshold of a new Golden Age - comparable to the Golden Age that Central City enjoyed after the second World War. This is a Golden Age we have been building up to since 1982, the year the Association fought its own war: The War of Accumulated Deficits."

The resolution of problems lay in four areas: the opera house, the properties, attendance figures, and the artistic and business condition.

Properties were now somewhat funded out of a bequest by Frank Ricketson, who died in June in his 92d year, barely remembered by anyone on the much-altered board, yet given acknowledgement in the 1987 program as "Mr. Central City Opera."

Attendance figures were gowing each season, evidence that the artistic direction was working closely with the business administration, too closely for imaginative programming, it seemed to some.

The 1987 season could hardly go wrong with *Madama Butterfly, Don Pasquale,* and *The Vagabond King*. The Friml musical was the major challenge and it turned out, despite Friml's beautiful songs, to be an unwieldy piece of operatic carpentry. Director Bill Gile seemed to wish to preserve every mouldy line, including all the awful 1920s humor. Every bit of excitement that baritone Parce created was undone by the clumsy theatricals of the interminable book. Severe cutting after the opening improved the pace but it was no hit like *The Desert Song*.

It said something about Moriarty's predictions for operetta that *The Vagabond King* was one of the few lacklustre productions of his boxoffice-conscious term.

Not so coincidentally, Santa Fe was also doing *Butterfly* in 1987, but this time Central City with a memorable Cio-Cio-San from Maryanne Telese, a vibrant Pinkerton from Don Bernardini, fresh direction from Roman Terleckyi, and John Moriarty's loving orchestral performance, led by a mile. The scale was ideal, and there were none of the inconsistencies that marred the Santa Fe production.

And for fun there was Central City's favorite comic opera, *Don Pasquale*. It had thrived in 1950, 1951, 1978, but seemed never such a comic lark as with Peter Strummer as the Don, Robert Orth as Malatesta, Sheryl Woods as Norina, and Gran Wilson as Ernesto. William Francisco was in rare comic form to direct these performers, and Mark Flint led the musical forces in an energetic, polished performance.

For 1987, Central City would report the highest box office revenues in its history: $480,000, with a 92 per cent average attendance, although *Madama Butterfly* registered 96.4 per cent of capacity.

In September the 1988 season was announced. Again there was to be *The Ballad of Baby Doe* in its sixth production. Amy Burton was the Baby Doe, Brian Steele the Tabor, and Dana Krueger the Augusta. Michael Ehrman directed with Moriarty conducting. It was well attended but considered dramatically deficient.

Verdi's *Macbeth* was new at Central City. Earnest efforts by David Holloway as Macbeth and Christine Seitz as his Lady were not enough to generate interest. Moriarty's musical leadership, Duain Wolfe's mighty chorus, Andrew Wentzel's splendid Banquo, and Don Bernardini's final act aria as Macduff made impressions far stronger than the whole. Roman Terlyckyi failed to stage the opera on the level of his 1987 *Butterfly*. Miguel Romero's contemporary-flavored sets provoked mild interest. The opera seemed not to belong at this house, and least of all in this production.

Sigmund Romberg's *The New Moon* was well cast with Maryanne Telese and Eric Allen Hanson. Smart stage direction by David Gately brought precision and tempo to the familiar. The tunes were lovely, the action improbable, and there was an amiable but gawkish atmosphere. It didn't make this a spectacular season.

Despite this, the 1988 season was a banner year for ticket sales which were 11 per cent higher than the 1987 season, reaching nearly $530,000.

The 1989 season had some surprises with the first ever presentation of Mozart's *The Magic Flute* and revivals of *Lucia di Lammermoor* and *The Desert Song*.

Not since 1975's *Don Giovanni* had there been Mozart at Central City. There had never been a Magic Flute in this opera house where Mozart operas are the vehicles of choice. Here the lightness and point of these operas thrive on the intimacy of the hall.

John Moriarty led a radiant orchestral performance in which James Michael Maguire, a former apprentice on the way up, was a nimble Papageno and Deborah Cole, yet another from the apprentice ranks, was a winsome Pamina. Gran Wilson was not in his best form as Tamino, his usually smooth delivery broken by spotty vocalism. Virginia Sublett was a fervent Queen of the Night, and Julian Rodescu was a woolly-voiced Sarastro.

David Gately devised simple-minded comedy that moved easily through Michael Anania's attractive, uncluttered sets. Gately did not carry through to achieve the nobility and humanity which marks the final scenes. The production seemed somewhat underpopulated; it was well received by audiences.

The strengths of Central City came into full bloom with the revival of Donizetti's *Lucia*. Karen Beardsley's Lucia was acute, assured, with a brilliance which encompassed lovely and sometimes hair-raising singing.

Musical director Brian Salesky and stage director Linda Brovsky and Beardsley had given careful thought to the production which resulted in a performance in which graceful and relevant movement on stage combined with ardent musicality in the pit for engrossing drama.

Don Bernardini was an able Edgardo, though evidence of vocal stress stood as warning to him to not push his voice. His characteristically sweet tone was too rare to lose. Eric Allen Hanson showed strength as the malevolent Enrico, and again Andrew Wentzel proved himself a vocal stalwart, one of Moriarty's best discoveries.

*The Desert Song* was even more fun this time around, for Dorothy Danner's direction found charming and funny details to pace the comedy, and Erich Parce again proved himself ideal in embracing both comic and romantic turns. Maryanne Telese brought class to the role of Margot, and conductor Duain Wolfe seemed to enjoy all the 1920s musical foolishness. Everyone brought style to the occasion - the style of the antic though tender twenties.

The seasons seemed to roll by smoothly, without the sense of crisis that had marked the 60s and 70s. Moriarty knew how to deal with the Board, how to produce successful seasons which kept the organization from jeopardy. If there were no strikingly creative productions, charged with excitement and originality, there was the evidence of such fine work as in *Lucia di Lammermoor*, the great zest of *Don Pasquale*, and the gusto of *The Barber of Seville*.

The 1990 season was billed as "A Season of Romance," and in it there would be *La Traviata, The Merry Widow*, and for refreshment the first production since 1948 of Mozart's *Cosi Fan Tutte*. The season were becoming almost predictable. Within exceedingly familiar territory, they were predictably well cast for the most part, ably conducted and staged.

The company was being carefully developed, and the best of the frequent performers, Sheryl Woods, Erich Parce, Maryanne Telese, Robert Orth, Karen Beardsley, Andrew Wentzel, and Eric Allen Hanson would honor any house.

The young singers being cultivated, Mark Calkins, Don Bernardini, Cynthia Lawrence, Susan Rosenbaum, and Joyce Campana, had marked potential which Moriarty explored with appropriate assignments.

There were singers he would like to have as regulars who were often unavailable, and chief among these was Janice Hall, the Aurora soprano who had done the 1980 Lucia with such imposing musicality. In 1990 she was one of the two Violettas;, but as a regional favorite was the one everyone wanted to hear. Candace Goetz was the alternate, and little was heard of her.

Adelaide Bishop, who had been the impish Adele, the fiery Norina, and a lesser Marguerite, came to direct the Traviata. There were no awkward moments in a pleasantly flowing presentation but there was no novelty in the production nor was there eccentricity.

Janice Hall had been building a strong career through five years as leading soprano in the Cologne Opera, and at Santa Fe had done Rosina in *The Barber*, Norina in *Don Pasquale*, and memorably, Dalinda, in its 1987 production of Handel's *Ariodante*.

As Violetta, she merged her radiant soprano with expressive acting to establish the character's vulnerability. There was a fine focus to her performance, with a deeply moving pathos in the final scene.

With superficial portrayals of Alfredo by Richard Estes and of Germont by Brian Steele, the soprano was without the strong support that would have made a truly superior production. Estes was movie-star pretty but seriously lacked vocal resonance, while Brian Steele was a one-dimensional baritone with loud notes.

There was exceptional grace and expressiveness to John Moriarty's conducting. The production utilized the still effective Richard Seger designs from the 1983 production. It was soprano Hall who quickened the pulse of the performance with her vivid imagination.

*Cosi Fan Tutte* was given theatrical pace both by stage director Jay Lesenger and conductor Brian Salesky. Casting was good with the exception of Kathleen Hegierski whose coarse Dorabella presented the character as a bobby-soxer from first to last.

Karen Beardsley had a coup as Despina, using her silvery soprano with ease and finding zestful comedy in the part. Andrew Wentzel was an exceptionally debonair Don Alfonso.

Jane Thorngren's plush soprano made her Fiordiligi a treat, and her handling of the two major arias showed dramatic sense and musicality. The two lovers, Gran Wilson as Ferrando and Eric Allen Hanson as Guglielmo, got entangled in some overly physical comedy but sang agreeably though Wilson was not up to previous form.

The production was another instance of scenery as banners to keep things light, and the production was attractively simple. If doing Mozart meant this sort of effort, one could adjust quite easily. The trick ending was funny though revisionist. Salesky seemed to have just the touch the music needed, and for him the orchestra played buoyantly.

As for *The Merry Widow*, it was the surest, most polished effort of the season, with the strongest cast, and the greatest lift to the musical performance under Michael Fardink. Lou Galterio's suave stage direction made this a wonderful refreshing of an operetta classic.

Marc Shulgold in the News found it "delightful - an operetta equivalent of Roger Rabbit." It was sold out before it opened, and in it there was more of Lehar's music than in the three previous versions.

The casting was special, with the always popular Robert Orth giving infectious joie de vivre to Danilo. Katherine Luna was new, a sadder but wiser and mature performer, with a fine range and beguiling presence.

Susan Rosenbaum was another Moriarty find, a mezzo of wit and beauty whose promise seemed exceptional, and she had been found among the apprentice artists, as had Mark Calkins, an apprentice in 1985 and 1986. His sweet lyric tenor was exactly right for Camille, completing an exceptional quartet of singers.

There were youth performances of *Cosi Fan Tutte* and *La Traviata*. Susan Rosenbaum was the Violetta, Richard Troxell the Alfredo, and Eric Graber the elder Germont. Children were admitted free; accompanying adults paid $5.

*The Face on the Barroom Floor* had only one performance in the Teller House Bar, but had eight performances in the Williams Stables across the way. One of the two alternating sopranos was Susan Rosenbaum. On ten different occasions, "Opera a la Carte" was offered in the Williams Stables, and included excerpts from Mozart, Rossini, and Offenbach. Also there were the Victorian Salon Recitals in the Teller House; these included a brunch, cost $17.50.

In January 1991 announcement was made of a campaign to raise $700,000 for capital improvements, including extension of the backstage, new handicap-accessible ladies and men's restrooms, a new costume shop, and a new roof for the flyloft. $150,000 had already been committed to these projects. New wiring and a computerized lighting system had been added in 1989.

The Association took pride in boasting that the Central City Opera had completed nine years in the black. It had been a long, hard road, and although some felt that innovative spirit had been lost along the way, no one could question the importance of this achievement.

In December 1990, a month following statewide approval of a gambling initiative for Central City, Black Hawk, and Cripple Creek, it was announced that the Board had given approval to a plan to offer limited gambling on the first floor of the Teller

House. It was said that anticipated taxes for the improvement of the Gilpin County infrastructure made this necessary.

Times were changing, and by the time the Festival had opened in 1992, the city was transformed from the old-time mining town into a place dedicated to gambling.

Gambling came to Central City like a ton of bricks dumped in its fragile lap.

There were casinos along Main Street and Eureka Street. They crept up towards the opera house. The Yellow Rose became a casino, the venerable Glory Hole took over a new and larger space and in enlarged digs became a casino. It had the wit to take along with it many of the wall signatures of performing artists of the late forties and fifties, and decorated an eating area with them.

A willing partner for the Teller House gambling operation was found by the Association in Tivolino, an Italian investor, which requested the authority to establish 120 slot machines, four poker tables, two blackjack tables, 15 video poker machines, and 15 blackjack machines. Amidst the lure of easy winnings, the Association could not be an ostrich. City planner Mike Matzko thought that by September 1992 there might be as many as 6,462 gambling devices in the town.

The Board had not been in favor of gambling, and worked quietly to oppose the passage of gambling legalization for Central City and Black Hawk. The other side of the coin was that there might be benefits from all the money that was flowing in and out of town. In the News, Marc Shulgold quoted a state gaming spokesman as saying that what had turned out to be 433 slot machines in the Teller House provided a daily take of $44,000.

An immediate plan was to use this new income to construct a four-room rehearsal hall on the site of the McFarlane Foundry, up the hill from the opera house, a $2 million investment in the opera's future, and always convertible to gaming should there be a fall in the Association's cultural fortunes.

The exchange was evident throughout town. Art galleries and souvenir shops and the few eating places had given way to slot machines. The Little Kingdom, where lead singers from the opera would come after performances to sing and mix with late-staying members of the audience, now was an unsocial space, loaded with what had once been called "one-arm bandits." The same destruction had been suffered by the Face bar, and certainly no more performances of the *Face on the Barroom Floor* would take place there.

Getting to Central City had become drudgery with constant streams of cars on the highways, and bumper-to-bumper traffic from Black Hawk to Central City. The Association leased land above the city's main parking lot, and ran shuttle buses for those going to the opera.

Just what the future might hold was difficult to see. Times had changed in Central City more than could have been imagined. How would this affect attendance at the opera and what would be done on stage. Would the newly won customers stay the course?

With new wealth could some risks be taken. Could there be a return to the excitement and innovations of the composers-in-residence programs which recognized the vitality of contemporary opera. These had been costly but gave the Association a forward stance. There never had been sufficient funding for such a program, but now funds might be available. But would there be audiences?

Could any serious effort at opera exist within this money-mad circumstance?

At the end of the 1992 season, general manager Daniel Rule admitted there was a 15 per cent drop in ticket sales, and also spoke of being approached by other non-gaming, mountain towns to move the opera there. There had been a formal letter from the Estes Park City Council, and Georgetown was mentioned in passing.

Just when finances had been brought under control, the gambling infusion sent land values roaring upwards. The Association's holdings now were valued at $20 million. Its tax bill was a commensurate $100,000 from which exemption was sought on the basis of its non-profit status. Some may have regretted selling off the key properties, but without that action, the Association might not have survived. But was it going to survive this latest onslaught?

* * * * *

In November 1991, it was announced that Beverly Sills would host a 60th Central City anniversary gala at the new Buell Theater in June 1992, and that Gran Wilson and Dominic Cossa would co-chair a committee to line up singers for this occasion.

An astonishing 56 years of actual operatic activity was being celebrated, since for four years during World War II no Festivals were held. That was not such a bad record of continuity.

There was some trepidation when it was announced that Christopher Sarson, producer of the tasteless melange which served as the grand opener of the Buell Theater early in November, would be its producer.

But the sight of the stage, in Robert Darling's lovely design, with yellow roses cascading along a trellis proscenium containing the classic Robert Edmond Jones curtain, was enough to move the ordinarily insensitive. A flight of kitchen chairs, such as provide seating in the opera house, hung high above the stage, and Central City billboards proclaiming Ruth Gordon in *A Doll's House*, Julie Harris in *The Lark*, and Myrna Loy in *Barefoot in the Park* were further nudges towards nostalgia.

Beverly Sills read an endearing letter from Lillian Gish in which she told of being called and asked by Margaret Harrington, the noted vocal coach, to come to Central City for *Camille*. To Lillian Gish, Margaret Carrington extolled Central City, the opera house, the opportunity, and those who would be involved in such an excited manner that when Lillian Gish hung up and repeated to her mother what she had just heard, her mother told her, "I didn't know that Miss Carrington drank."

Of greatest concern to Lilian Gish was that the Central City Opera House be "preserved and cherished."

There were waves of nostalgia as Janice Hall sang "I Dreamt I Dwelt in Marble Halls," from *The Bohemian Girl*, the operetta so popular in its two performances at the Belvidere in 1874 that it started the wheels rolling for construction of the new opera house.

A grand gathering of singers past and present was there. None evoked more admiration than 71-year old Jerome Hines, straight as a ramrod and singing with an ultimate power and control.

There was an extraordinary gathering of the talents that had been involved in the 1956 premiere of *The Ballad of Baby Doe*, with Walter Cassel, its born-to-the-part Tabor; Beverly Sills who in New York though not at Central City made Baby Doe her first great role; and Frances Bible, the incomparable Augusta. Though Cassel and Sills no longer sing, Bible does, though not on this occasion.

It was David Holloway who sang Tabor in the reenactment of the final scene, with Cynthia Lawrence as Baby Doe, and Dana Krueger as Augusta.

Sheryl Woods and Robert Orth brought the kind of buoyancy that has marked to many Central City seasons to a duet from *Don Pasquale*. Erich Parce sang from *The Desert Song* with an inspired romantic lunacy. A large number of 1992 apprentices took part, underscoring the program which for over forty years has turned out singers of such quality as Samuel Ramey, David Holloway, Richard Cowan, J. Patrick Raftery, James Michael Maguire, and Katherine Ciesinski.

The evening was capped by Cynthia Lawrence, another former apprentice, who brought beauty of spirit and tone to the singing of Baby Doe's final scene, in which she affirms her dedication to watching over the Matchless Mine until eternity.

Past, present, and future came together with taste and the magic of music to make this event one to "preserve and cherish" as Lillian Gish had put it.

\*   \*   \*   \*   \*

Moriarty hoped for a "Golden Age" for opera at Central City, and by demanding all-round proficiency he was ensuring stability. He referred to the post-World War II period at Central City as a "Golden Age," and under Frank St. Leger's overall direction, with Emil Cooper, the finest of all Central City conductors, Herbert Graf with his strong directorial hand, and Donald Oenslager, the master of stage design, this was not an exaggeration.

Then, daring or not, Beethoven's *Fidelio* was performed, and the first glittering performance of *Cosi Fan Tutte*. In preparation for a Met production, Mozart's *The Abduction from the Seraglio* was performed with then little known Eleanor Steber. In 1948, Offenbach's *The Tales of Hoffman* was also little known, but it was a hit which introduced Jerome Hines and sent the opera on to current popularity.

In early June, weeks before the start of the season, Moriarty announced the 1991 and 1992 seasons. For 1991 there would be *Die Fledermaus* in its fifth production; *Tosca* in its third production; and Gounod's *Romeo and Juliet* for the first time since 1951.

In 1992, *Faust* for the first time since 1954; Rossini's *The Italian Girl in Algiers*, for the first time since 1954, and Romberg's The *Student Prince* seen once in 1984, made an uneven menu.

While the Rossini was welcomed, the two Gounod operas, done in advance of the 100th anniversary of his death in 1893, made an unexciting observation of the fact. There was no Mozart or Donizetti or anything remotely contemporary.

In 1993, the sure fire *Carmen, Falstaff*, a stranger since 1973, and a first-time Friml *Rose Marie* would be done.

Musical-theatrical experiences like the ingratiating *Fables*, the searingly magnificent *Of Mice and Men*, and the provocative *Postcards from Morocco* were not encountered in this conservative period in which there was much to conserve.

There was unmistakably the touch of success in the financial and organizational security which accompanied the presentation of Old Favorites.

In 1957 I wrote in The Lively Arts that "Those who lead today (in the Central City Opera House Association) are heading a huge entitity from which both artistic and financial returns must be drawn. Central City is big business, a big investment, but still biggest when most artistically worthy.

"The national prestige which Central City has drawn from premiering *The Ballad of Baby Doe*, and from beating the Met to make hits of Mozart's *Cosi Fan Tutte* and Donizetti's *Don Pasquale* has brought to Colorado some of its most rewarding visitors. They too have taken from Colorado 'the things that last when gold is gone.' Praise in the press and by word of mouth keeps Central City alive across the nation."

"In short 1958 finds Central City sitting back safely, failing to exercise the 'daring and imagination' which constantly refreshed the enterprise in its early years. Now is the time to start thinking of 1959, of doing one of those marvelously engaging Rossini or Donizetti operas, Mozart's *Don Giovanni*, Wolfe-Ferrari's *The Four Ruffians*, or a new opera such as Carlisle Floyd's *Susannah*, the Menotti-Barber *Vanessa*, or something perhaps yet to be written."

It was Anne Evans who had spoken of "... the things that last when gold is gone. The miners wanted the riches of life, they wanted entertainment, and they wanted the best, for their daring and imagination was of the stuff that makes and demands good theater."

The 1990s were not in the best sense conservative. They pulled away from anything that inferred experimentation or novelty. The Central City Opera had built an audience which relished the opportunity to escape from the problems of the times. In this period house there have been miracles of song, moments of lyrical magic, and others of dramatic grandeur which have encompassed four centuries of operatic endeavor.

Opera had been brought to life on this tiny stage with enviable resourcefulness. It was up to audiences to match this with an increased awareness and insight. What was needed was a serious commitment to take opera seriously by producers and audiences.

Changing times and values might not permit Central City's opera house or its audiences to perform this role. Unchanging attitudes and the greatly altered environment of Central City might decide on their own.

# REPERTORY
## CENTRAL CITY OPERA HOUSE

1932
CAMILLE

1933
THE MERRY WIDOW

1934
OTHELLO

1935
CENTRAL CITY NIGHTS

1936
THE GONDOLIERS

1937
A DOLL'S HOUSE

1938
RUY BLAS

1939
THE YEOMAN OF THE GUARD

1940
THE BARTERED BRIDE

1941
THE BARBER OF SEVILLE
ORPHEUS

1942 - 1946
Dark

1946
LA TRAVIATA
THE ABDUCTION FROM THE SERAGLIO

1947
FIDELIO
MARTHA
HARVEY

1948
THE TALES OF HOFFMAN
COSI FAN TUTTE
THE PLAY'S THE THING

1949
DIE FLEDERMAUS
DIAMOND LIL

1950
MADAMA BUTTERFLY
DON PASQUALE
THE DEVIL'S DISCIPLE

1951
ROMEO AND JULIET
DON PASQUALE
THE BEAUTIFUL GALATEA
AMELIA GOES TO THE BALL
THE CONSTANT WIFE

1952
LA BOHEME
THE MARRIAGE OF FIGARO
MRS. MCTHING

1953
CARMEN
THE MERRY WIVES OF WINDSOR
THE TIME OF THE CUCKOO

1954
FAUST
ARIADNE AUF NAXOS
THE CAINE MUTINY COURT MARTIAL

1955
THE MIKADO
HMS PINAFORE
TRIAL BY JURY
THE YEOMAN OF THE GUARD
IOLANTHE
BUS STOP

1956
THE BALLAD OF BABY DOE
LA TOSCA
THE LARK

1957
RIGOLETTO
THE GYPSY BARON
SEPARATE TABLES

1958
LA PERICHOLE
CAVALLERIA RUSTICANA
I PAGLIACCI
AND PERHAPS HAPPINESS

1959
DIE FLEDERMAUS
THE BALLAD OF BABY DOE
THE GAZEBO

1960
LUCIA DI LAMMERMOOR
AIDA
A THURBER CARNIVAL

1961
THE ELIXIR OF LOVE
LA TRAVIATA
THE MIRACLE WORKER

1962
THE GIRL OF THE GOLDEN WEST
LA BOHEME
MARY, MARY

1963
DON GIOVANNI
IL TROVATORE
NEVER TOO LATE

1964
MADAMA BUTTERFLY
THE LADY FROM COLORADO
BAREFOOT IN THE PARK

1965
MANON
LAKME
THE BARBER OF SEVILLE
ANY WEDNESDAY

1966
CARMEN
THE BALLAD OF BABY DOE
THE ITALIAN GIRL IN ALGIERS
THE ODD COUPLE

1967
THE MERRY WIDOW
A MASKED BALL
DON PASQUALE
CACTUS FLOWER

1968
HMS PINAFORE
THE YEOMAN OF THE GUARD
THE MIKADO
THE PIRATES OF PENZANCE
THERE'S A GIRL IN MY SOUP

1969
DIE FLEDERMAUS
TOSCA
PLAZA SUITE

1970
LA BOHEME
OF MICE AND MEN
FORTY CARATS

1971
I DO! I DO!
LILLIAN GISH AND THE MOVIES
Max Morath

1972
THE MARRIAGE OF FIGARO
FALSTAFF
1776
LAST OF THE RED HOT LOVERS
PRIVATE LIVES

1973
FALSTAFF
THE BARBER OF SEVILLE
THE GERSHWIN YEARS
THE HOLLOW CROWN
THE IRREGULAR VERB TO LOVE

1974
A MIDSUMMER NIGHT'S DREAM
RIGOLETTO
GIGI

1975
DON GIOVANNI
SCIPIO AFRICANUS
AIDA (In Denver)

1976
THE BALLAD OF BABY DOE
LA BOHEME (In Denver)

1977
THE BARTERED BRIDE
A MIDSUMMER NIGHT'S DREAM
Anna Russell

1978
SALOME (In Denver)
THE BOHEMIAN GIRL
DON PASQUALE
THE FACE ON THE BARROOM FLOOR

1979
THE MERRY WIDOW
THE BARBER OF SEVILLE
THE MEDIUM
SOYAZHE
THE CIRCLE
A MONTH IN THE COUNTRY

1980
CANDIDE
LUCIA DI LAMMERMOOR
POSTCARD FROM MOROCCO
HAY FEVER
BURIED CHILD

1981
THE BALLAD OF BABY DOE
MADAMA BUTTERFLY
FABLES

1982
Dark

1983
LA TRAVIATA
THE ELIXIR OF LOVE

1984
RIGOLETTO
CINDERELLA
THE STUDENT PRINCE

1985
CARMEN
THE DAUGHTER OF THE REGIMENT
THE DESERT SONG

1986
LA BOHEME
THE BARBER OF SEVILLE
NAUGHTY MARIETTA

1987
MADAMA BUTTERFLY
DON PASQUALE
THE VAGABOND KING

1988
THE BALLAD OF BABY DOE
MACBETH
THE NEW MOON

1989
THE MAGIC FLUTE
LUCIA DI LAMMERMOOR
THE DESERT SONG

1990
LA TRAVIATA
THE MERRY WIDOW
COSI FAN TUTTE

1991
DIE FLEDERMAUS
TOSCA
ROMEO AND JULIET

1992
FAUST
THE ITALIAN GIRL IN ALGIERS
THE STUDENT PRINCE

1993
ROSE MARIE
CARMEN
FALSTAFF